FROM ZERO
TO HERO IN R

Transform the Way You
See and Understand Data

Alexander J. Smith

Table of Contents

CHAPTER 1

Getting Started with R

R is a powerful language and environment for statistical computing and graphics. It is highly extensible and provides a wide variety of statistical and graphical techniques. To embark on your journey with R, the first step is installing R and RStudio, a popular integrated development environment (IDE) that makes using R much easier.

To install R, visit the Comprehensive R Archive Network (CRAN) at `https://cran.r-project.org/` and select the version appropriate for your operating system. Follow the installation instructions provided on the site. After installing R, the next step is to install RStudio, which can be downloaded from `https://www.rstudio.com/`. Choose the free version, RStudio Desktop, and follow the installation guide.

Once both R and RStudio are installed, launch RStudio to get started. You will see an interface divided into several areas: the Console, where you can type R commands and see their output; the Environment/History pane, showing your current work environment and command history; the Files/Plots/Packages/Help/Viewer pane, where you can navigate through your files, see plots, manage packages, and access help documentation.

Before diving into data analysis, familiarize yourself with basic R syntax. R syntax is the set of rules that defines how programs are written in R. Here are a few basic operations to get you started:

- **Arithmetic Operations**: You can perform basic arithmetic operations like addition (+), subtraction (-), multiplication (*), and division (/). For example, to add two numbers, you would type `2 + 2` in the console and press Enter.

- **Logical Operations**: R supports logical operations such as greater than (>), less than (<), equal to (==), and not equal to (!=). For instance, to check if five is greater than two, you would type `5 > 2`.

Understanding data types and structures is crucial in R. The basic data types include numeric, character, and logical. Data structures include vectors, matrices, lists, and data frames, each serving different purposes in data analysis.

- **Vectors** are the simplest type of data structure in R. A vector can contain multiple elements of the same data type. Create a vector using the `c()` function, like `c(1, 2, 3, 4, 5)`.

- **Data Frames** are used to store tabular data. They are similar to matrices but can contain different types of data in each column. Use the `data.frame()` function to create a data frame.

This foundational knowledge will set the stage for more advanced data manipulation and analysis techniques covered in later chapters.

Introduction to R and Its Environment

R's environment is a comprehensive ecosystem that includes the R language itself, various Integrated Development Environments (IDEs) like RStudio, and a vast array of packages available through the Comprehensive R Archive Network (CRAN). Understanding this environment is crucial for effective data analysis and visualization.

At the heart of R's environment is the **CRAN**, which serves as the main repository for R packages. These packages extend R's capabilities, allowing users to perform a wide range of statistical analyses and graphical representations. To install a package from CRAN, you can use the `install.packages()` function directly in the R console. For example, to install the `ggplot2` package, you would run:

```R
install.packages("ggplot2")
```

After installation, you must load the package into your R session to use it. This is done with the `library()` function:

```R
library(ggplot2)
```

RStudio enhances R's environment by providing an organized workspace that includes a script editor, console, and tools for plotting, history, debugging, and workspace management. It's particularly favored for its user-friendly interface and additional features that facilitate coding in R. RStudio also supports R Markdown, a dynamic document format that allows you to run R code within markdown documents, making it easier to share analyses with non-programmers.

Another critical aspect of R's environment is its comprehensive help system. R and all CRAN packages come with documentation accessible using the `help()` function or the `?` operator. For instance, to get help on the `plot` function, you could type:

```R
help(plot)
```

or

```R
?plot
```

This documentation includes descriptions of the function's purpose, its arguments, and examples of how to use it. Additionally, the `example()` function can run example code from the documentation, providing a hands-on way to learn:

```R
example(plot)
```

R's environment is also highly customizable. Users can tailor their workspace in RStudio, choose from various packages to suit their project's needs, and even write their own functions to perform specific tasks. The ability to script in R allows for automating repetitive tasks, making data analysis more efficient.

Understanding and navigating R's environment is foundational for anyone looking to perform data analysis or statistical computing. With its combination of powerful tools, extensive packages, and supportive documentation, R's environment is designed to help users from various backgrounds transform their data into actionable insights.

Installing R and RStudio

After successfully installing R from the Comprehensive R Archive Network (CRAN), the next crucial step is to install RStudio, which significantly enhances the R programming experience. RStudio is an Integrated Development Environment (IDE) that provides a user-friendly interface for coding, debugging, and visualizing data in R. Here's a detailed guide to installing RStudio:

1. **Navigate to the RStudio Download Page**: Open your web browser and go to `https://www.rstudio.com/products/rstudio/download/`. This page lists various versions of RStudio, including RStudio Desktop and RStudio Server. For most users, especially those new to R, RStudio Desktop is the recommended choice.

2. **Select the Right Version**: Choose RStudio Desktop and click on the download link for the version compatible with your operating system (Windows, Mac, or Linux).

3. **Download and Install**: Click on the installer file to download it. Once the download is complete, run the installer. Follow the on-screen instructions to complete the installation process. The installer will guide you through the necessary steps, which typically include agreeing to the license, selecting an installation directory, and confirming the installation.

4. **Launch RStudio**: After installation, open RStudio just like any other application on your computer. Upon launching, you'll be greeted with the RStudio interface, which is divided into several panels for the console, script editor, environment/history, and files/plots/packages/help.

5. **Configure Your Workspace**: Although RStudio works well with default settings, you might want to customize your workspace. Go to `Tools > Global Options` to explore various settings, such as appearance (themes, font size), code editing options (tab size, soft wrap), and more. Adjust these settings according to your preference to optimize your workflow.

6. **Test Your Installation**: To ensure that both R and RStudio are installed correctly, try running a simple command in the RStudio console. For example, type `print("Hello,`

`R!")` and press Enter. If you see `[1]` `"Hello, R!"` as the output, congratulations! You've successfully set up R and RStudio on your computer.

By following these steps, you've laid the foundation for your journey into data analysis and visualization with R. RStudio will serve as your companion, simplifying the coding process and providing powerful tools for your data science projects.

Basic R Syntax and Operations

In R, understanding the **basic syntax and operations** is crucial for performing data analysis and visualization effectively. This section delves into the foundational aspects that will empower you to manipulate data and execute various operations with confidence.

Variables and Assignment: In R, variables are used to store data values. The assignment operator <- is commonly used to assign values to variables. For example, to assign the value 10 to a variable named x, you would write:

```R
x <- 10
```

This operation stores the integer 10 in the variable x. You can also use the = operator for assignment, but <- is preferred in the R community for its clarity and tradition.

Functions and Arguments: Functions are predefined commands that perform specific tasks in R. They take inputs, called arguments, and return an output. For instance, the sum() function calculates the sum of its arguments. To add the numbers 5 and 3, you would call the sum() function with 5 and 3 as its arguments:

```R
sum(5, 3)
```

This returns 8, the sum of 5 and 3.

Data Types: R supports various data types, including:

- **Numeric**: Represents decimal values as well as integers. For example, 42 or 3.14.

- **Character**: Represents strings of text. Character strings are enclosed in quotes, such as `"Hello, world!"`.

- **Logical**: Represents boolean values, `TRUE` or `FALSE`.

Understanding these data types is essential for data manipulation and condition testing in R.

Control Structures: Control structures allow you to control the flow of execution in your R scripts. The most common structures include `if`, `else`, and `for` loops.

- An `if` statement might check if a number is positive and print a message accordingly:

```R
number <- -3
if (number > 0) {
  print("Positive number")
} else {
  print("Non-positive number")
}
```

- A `for` loop allows you to iterate over a sequence. For example, to print numbers 1 through 5:

```R
for (i in 1:5) {
  print(i)
}
```

Vectorization: One of R's strengths is its ability to operate on entire vectors of data at once without the need for explicit looping. For example, adding two vectors together combines each corresponding element:

```R
v1 <- c(1, 2, 3)
v2 <- c(4, 5, 6)
sum <- v1 + v2
```

This results in sum holding the value c(5, 7, 9), demonstrating how operations can be applied element-wise across vectors.

Subsetting: Extracting specific elements from vectors, matrices, or data frames is a common task. For vectors, you can use square brackets [] to specify the indices of the elements you wish to extract:

```R
v <- c(10, 20, 30, 40, 50)
v[2] # Extracts the second element, resulting in 20
v[c(1, 3)] # Extracts the first and third elements, resulting in
c(10, 30)
```

For data frames, you can extract columns by name using the $ operator:

```R
df <- data.frame(Name = c("Alice", "Bob"), Age = c(25, 30))
df$Name # Extracts the "Name" column
```

Logical Operations and Filtering: Logical operators allow you to test conditions and filter data based on those conditions. For example, to find elements of a vector that are greater than 20:

```R
v <- c(10, 20, 30, 40, 50)
v[v > 20]
```

This returns c(30, 40, 50), the elements of v that satisfy the condition v > 20.

By mastering these basic syntax and operations, you'll be well-equipped to tackle more complex data analysis tasks in R. Each concept introduced here serves as a building block for the advanced techniques discussed in later chapters, enabling you to transform and analyze your data with greater efficiency and insight.

Arithmetic Operations

In R, arithmetic operations are fundamental to data analysis, allowing you to perform calculations on your data. These operations include addition, subtraction, multiplication, and division, each represented by +, -, *, and / respectively. For instance, to calculate the sum of 8 and 4, you would use the expression 8 + 4, which yields 12. Similarly, to find the difference, product, or quotient of the same numbers, you would use 8 - 4, 8 * 4, and 8 / 4, resulting in 4, 32, and 2, respectively.

Beyond these basic operations, R also supports more complex mathematical functions such as exponentiation and square root, represented by ^ and sqrt() respectively. For example, raising 2 to the power of 3 is achieved by 2 ^ 3, giving 8 as the result. To find the square root of 16, you would use sqrt(16), which returns 4.

R's ability to handle arithmetic operations extends to vectors and matrices, allowing for element-wise calculations. When performing operations on vectors of the same length, R applies the operation to each corresponding pair of elements. For example, given two vectors v1 <- c(1, 2, 3) and v2 <- c(4, 5, 6), adding them together with v1 + v2 yields c(5, 7, 9). This principle applies to subtraction, multiplication, and division as well.

When working with matrices, these operations are similarly straightforward. If m1 and m2 are matrices of the same dimensions, m1 + m2 will add the two matrices element-wise. It's important to ensure that the dimensions match to avoid errors.

For operations involving a single number and a vector or matrix, R broadcasts the number across the structure, performing the operation with each element. For instance, adding 2 to a vector v <- c(1, 2, 3) with v + 2 results in c(3, 4, 5).

Understanding and utilizing these arithmetic operations is crucial for data manipulation in R. They form the basis for more advanced analytical tasks, enabling you to prepare and transform your data effectively for analysis.

Logical Operations

Logical operations in R are essential for making decisions and controlling the flow of execution in your scripts. These operations evaluate expressions and return boolean values: TRUE or FALSE. Understanding how to use these operations effectively is crucial for filtering data, performing conditional execution, and more complex data manipulation tasks.

R supports several logical operators:

- **AND** (`&`): Returns TRUE if both operands are TRUE.

- **OR** (`|`): Returns TRUE if at least one of the operands is TRUE.

- **NOT** (`!`): Returns TRUE if the operand is FALSE.

Let's explore each operator with examples to illustrate their use.

AND Operator

The `&` operator checks if both conditions on its sides are TRUE. For instance, to check if a number is greater than 5 and less than 10, you could write:

```R
number <- 7
result <- (number > 5) & (number < 10)
print(result) # Outputs: [1] TRUE
```

OR Operator

The `|` operator checks if at least one condition on its sides is TRUE. It's useful when you have multiple conditions that could satisfy a requirement. For example, to check if a number is either less than 2 or greater than 8:

```R
number <- 9
result <- (number < 2) | (number > 8)
print(result) # Outputs: [1] TRUE
```

NOT Operator

The `!` operator inverts the truth value of its operand. If the condition is TRUE, using `!` will make it FALSE, and vice versa. This operator is particularly useful in filtering data. For example, to select items that are not equal to a specified value:

```R
```

```
value <- 5
result <- !(value == 5)
print(result) # Outputs: [1] FALSE
```

Combining Logical Operators

Logical operators can be combined to form more complex conditions. When doing so, it's important to use parentheses to group conditions and control the order of evaluation. For example, to check if a number is either less than 5 or greater than 10, but not equal to 7:

R
```
number <- 11
result <- ((number < 5) | (number > 10)) & !(number == 7)
print(result) # Outputs: [1] TRUE
```

Working with Vectors

Logical operations can also be applied to vectors, producing a vector of logical values. This feature is particularly powerful for subsetting data. For instance, to find the elements of a vector that are greater than 5:

R
```
numbers <- c(2, 4, 6, 8)
result <- numbers > 5
print(result) # Outputs: [1] FALSE FALSE TRUE TRUE
```

You can then use this logical vector to subset the original vector:

R
```
filtered_numbers <- numbers[numbers > 5]
print(filtered_numbers) # Outputs: [1] 6 8
```

Understanding and utilizing logical operations in R allows you to perform sophisticated data manipulation and analysis tasks. By mastering these operators, you can write more efficient and powerful R scripts, enabling you to filter and analyze your data with greater precision.

Understanding Data Types and Structures

In R, data types and structures form the backbone of data analysis and visualization. Grasping these concepts is crucial for manipulating and understanding your data effectively. Let's delve into the core data types and structures you'll encounter in R.

Data Types:

1. **Numeric**: This is the default type for numbers in R. Numeric data can be either integer (e.g., 2L, where `L` denotes an integer) or double (e.g., 2.5).

2. **Character**: Any text or string values are considered character types. For example, `"Hello, World!"`.

3. **Logical**: This type represents boolean values and can be either `TRUE` or `FALSE`.

4. **Complex**: For complex numbers with real and imaginary parts, e.g., `1+4i`.

5. **Raw**: Intended to hold raw bytes.

Data Structures:

1. **Vectors**: The simplest and most common data structure in R. A vector holds elements of the same data type. Use the `c()` function to create vectors, e.g., `c(1, 2, 3)` for a numeric vector or `c("a", "b", "c")` for a character vector.

2. **Matrices**: Two-dimensional, rectangular data structures that can store data of a single type. Create matrices with the `matrix()` function, specifying the number of rows and columns.

3. **Arrays**: Similar to matrices but can have more than two dimensions. Use the `array()` function, specifying the data and a dimension vector.

4. **Data Frames**: More complex than matrices, data frames can hold columns of different types. They are crucial for data analysis in R. Create data frames with the `data.frame()` function, e.g., `data.frame(Column1 = c(1, 2), Column2 = c("a", "b"))`.

5. **Lists**: An ordered collection that can contain objects of different types and structures. Lists are created using the `list()` function, e.g., `list(Number = 42, Name = "R", Data = 1:10)`.

Understanding these data types and structures is fundamental for data manipulation in R. For example, when working with datasets, knowing whether your data should be handled as a vector, matrix, or data frame can significantly affect your analysis's outcome. Similarly, recognizing the data type you're working with helps determine the appropriate functions and operations to apply, ensuring accuracy and efficiency in your work.

To practice, try creating each data type and structure with the examples provided, and explore the functions associated with each. For instance, investigate functions like `str()` to understand the structure of an object, or `class()` to determine an object's type. Experimenting with these will solidify your understanding and prepare you for more advanced data manipulation and analysis tasks in R.

Vectors and Matrices

Vectors and matrices are foundational to working with data in R, allowing for efficient storage and manipulation of numerical and categorical data sets. Understanding how to create, access, and manipulate these structures is essential for any data analysis task.

Vectors in R are created using the `c()` function, which stands for concatenate. This function combines values into a vector. For instance, to create a numeric vector containing the numbers 1 through 5, you would use:

```r
numeric_vector <- c(1, 2, 3, 4, 5)
```

Similarly, to create a character vector containing the first three letters of the alphabet, you would use:

```r
character_vector <- c("a", "b", "c")
```

It's important to note that vectors in R are homogeneous, meaning all elements must be of the same data type. If you combine different types, R will coerce them to a common type, with character types taking precedence over numeric types.

Matrices are two-dimensional data structures, where data is organized into rows and columns. To create a matrix, you can use the `matrix()` function, specifying the data, the number of rows, and the number of columns. Optionally, you can also specify whether the matrix should be filled by row or by column (the default). For example, to create a 3x3 matrix with numbers 1 through 9, you would use:

```r
matrix_data <- matrix(1:9, nrow = 3, ncol = 3)
```

Accessing elements within vectors and matrices is straightforward. For vectors, you simply specify the index of the element you wish to access in square brackets. For matrices, you specify the row and column of the element you wish to access, separated by a comma. For example, to access the second element of `numeric_vector` and the element in the second row, third column of `matrix_data`, you would use:

```r
numeric_vector[2]
matrix_data[2, 3]
```

Manipulating these structures is also intuitive. For vectors, you can add elements using the `c()` function again, or change elements by specifying their index. For matrices, you can add rows or columns using the `rbind()` and `cbind()` functions, respectively. For example, to add a value to `numeric_vector` and a column to `matrix_data`, you would use:

```r
numeric_vector <- c(numeric_vector, 6)
new_column <- matrix(c(10, 11, 12), nrow = 3)
matrix_data <- cbind(matrix_data, new_column)
```

Understanding and mastering vectors and matrices are crucial steps in becoming proficient in data manipulation and analysis in R. These structures are not only fundamental to the R language but also provide a solid foundation for understanding more complex data types and structures you will encounter as you delve deeper into data analysis.

Lists and Data Frames

Lists in R are among the most versatile data structures, allowing you to store a collection of objects under a single name. Each element within a list can be of any type, including numbers, strings, vectors, and even other lists. This flexibility makes lists incredibly useful for organizing and managing complex data structures. To create a list, use the `list()` function, specifying the elements you wish to include. For example, to create a list containing a numeric vector, a character string, and a matrix, you could use the following code:

r

```
my_list <- list(NumericVector = c(1, 2, 3), CharacterString = "R is
amazing", Matrix = matrix(1:9, nrow = 3))
```

One of the key features of lists is that you can access and modify their components using the list name followed by the `$` operator and the component name. For instance, to access the `NumericVector` component of `my_list`, you would use `my_list$NumericVector`. This aspect of lists makes them highly dynamic and adaptable to various data manipulation tasks.

Data frames, on the other hand, are used to store tabular data in R. They are similar to matrices in that data is organized into rows and columns, but unlike matrices, each column in a data frame can contain different types of data. This makes data frames particularly suited for statistical modeling and data analysis, where datasets often contain a mix of numeric, categorical, and text data. To create a data frame, use the `data.frame()` function, specifying each column as a vector of data. For example:

r

```
my_data_frame <- data.frame(ID = 1:3, Name = c("Alice", "Bob",
"Charlie"), Score = c(90, 85, 88))
```

In this data frame, `ID` and `Score` are numeric vectors, while `Name` is a character vector. Accessing and manipulating data within a data frame is straightforward. You can use the `$` operator to access a column by name, similar to how you would access components of a list. For example, `my_data_frame$Name` would return the `Name` column from `my_data_frame`.

Both lists and data frames can be manipulated using a variety of functions in R. For lists, functions like `lapply()` and `sapply()` are particularly useful for applying a function to each component of the list. For data frames, the `dplyr` package provides a powerful set of tools for data manipulation, including filtering, selecting, and summarizing data.

When working with lists and data frames, it's important to understand the structure of your data. The `str()` function can be invaluable here, providing a concise summary of the structure of an object. For example, running `str(my_list)` or `str(my_data_frame)` will give you a quick overview of the components of a list or the columns of a data frame, including the type of data each contains.

In practice, lists and data frames are foundational to data analysis in R. Whether you're organizing complex data structures in lists or managing datasets in data frames, mastering these data types will enhance your ability to manipulate and analyze data effectively. Experiment with creating and modifying lists and data frames, and explore the functions available for working with these structures. As you become more familiar with these data types, you'll find they offer a powerful toolkit for data analysis and visualization in R.

Basic Data Manipulation

In R, **basic data manipulation** encompasses a variety of operations that allow you to modify, subset, and interact with your data. Understanding these operations is crucial for effective data analysis. This section will cover several fundamental techniques, including subsetting data, merging and sorting datasets, which are essential skills in any data analyst's toolkit.

Subsetting Data

Subsetting refers to the process of extracting specific parts of your data based on certain conditions. In R, you can subset data using square brackets `[]`, the `subset()` function, or the `dplyr` package.

- **Using Square Brackets**: You can subset a vector, matrix, or data frame using square brackets. For a vector, `vector[index]` will return the element at the specified index. For a matrix or data frame, `data[row, column]` allows you to select by row and column numbers.

```r
# Subsetting a vector
my_vector <- c(1, 2, 3, 4, 5)
subset_vector <- my_vector[2:4]
# Subsetting a data frame
my_data_frame <- data.frame(ID = 1:5, Value = c("A", "B", "C", "D", "E"))
```

```
subset_data_frame <- my_data_frame[1:3, ]
```

- **Using the** `subset()` Function: The `subset()` function is particularly useful for data frames. It allows you to select rows that meet certain conditions and to choose which columns to return.

r

```
subset_data_frame <- subset(my_data_frame, ID <= 3, select = c(ID, Value))
```

- **Using** `dplyr` Package: The `dplyr` package provides a more intuitive syntax for subsetting and manipulating data. Functions like `filter()` and `select()` are used for subsetting rows and selecting columns, respectively.

r

```
library(dplyr)
filtered_data <- filter(my_data_frame, ID <= 3)
selected_data <- select(my_data_frame, ID, Value)
```

Merging Data

Merging data involves combining two datasets based on a common variable. The `merge()` function in R allows you to do this efficiently.

r

```
data_frame1 <- data.frame(ID = 1:3, Value1 = c("A", "B", "C"))
data_frame2 <- data.frame(ID = 2:4, Value2 = c("D", "E", "F"))
merged_data <- merge(data_frame1, data_frame2, by = "ID")
```

Sorting Data

Sorting your data can be crucial for analysis, making it easier to understand patterns and anomalies. In R, you can use the `order()` function to sort data frames.

r

```
sorted_data <- my_data_frame[order(my_data_frame$Value), ]
```

Additionally, the `arrange()` function from the `dplyr` package offers a straightforward way to sort data frames.

```r
library(dplyr)
sorted_data <- arrange(my_data_frame, Value)
```

These basic data manipulation techniques form the foundation of data analysis in R. By mastering subsetting, merging, and sorting, you can prepare your data for more complex analysis and visualization tasks. Experiment with these techniques using your own datasets to gain a deeper understanding and proficiency in data manipulation with R.

Subsetting Data

Subsetting data in R is a powerful technique that allows you to extract portions of your dataset that meet specific criteria, enabling focused analysis on relevant data points. This process can be applied to vectors, matrices, and data frames, each requiring a slightly different approach due to their unique structures. Understanding how to effectively subset data is crucial for any data analysis task, as it allows you to manipulate and analyze subsets of your data efficiently.

For vectors, subsetting is straightforward. You use square brackets `[]` to specify the indices of the elements you want to extract. For example, if you have a numeric vector `numbers` and you want to extract the first, third, and fifth elements, you would use the following code:

```r
numbers <- c(10, 20, 30, 40, 50)
subset_numbers <- numbers[c(1, 3, 5)]
```

This technique is not limited to numeric vectors; it applies to character vectors and logical vectors as well. The key is to specify the correct indices within the square brackets.

When working with matrices, subsetting becomes a bit more complex because you have to consider both rows and columns. To subset a matrix, you use a comma within the square brackets to separate row indices from column indices. For instance, if you have a matrix `data_matrix` and you want to extract the elements from the first two rows and the first two columns, you would use:

r

```r
data_matrix <- matrix(1:9, nrow = 3)
subset_matrix <- data_matrix[1:2, 1:2]
```

This code snippet extracts a smaller matrix consisting of the first two rows and columns from the original matrix. You can also use the `drop = FALSE` argument to ensure that the result retains its matrix structure, even if it's technically a vector or a single value.

Data frames, which are arguably the most commonly used data structure in R for data analysis, require a more nuanced approach to subsetting. You can subset data frames by rows, columns, or both, using indices, names, or logical vectors. For example, to extract the first three rows from a data frame `df`, you would use:

r

```r
subset_df_rows <- df[1:3, ]
```

To extract specific columns by name, you can use:

r

```r
subset_df_columns <- df[, c("ColumnName1", "ColumnName2")]
```

Moreover, the `subset()` function offers a more intuitive way to subset data frames based on conditions. For instance, to extract rows where the value in the `Age` column is greater than 30, you could use:

r

```r
subset_df_condition <- subset(df, Age > 30)
```

The `dplyr` package further simplifies subsetting and manipulating data frames with functions like `filter()` for subsetting rows based on conditions and `select()` for choosing columns. Using `dplyr`, the previous example can be rewritten as:

r

```r
library(dplyr)
```

```
subset_df_condition <- filter(df, Age > 30)
```

Subsetting is not just about extracting data; it's about focusing your analysis on the data that matters. Whether you're working with simple vectors or complex data frames, mastering subsetting allows you to navigate your datasets more effectively, leading to more insightful analyses. As you practice these techniques, consider the structure of your data and the specific subsets you need to extract to answer your analytical questions. Remember, the goal of subsetting is to make your data analysis tasks more manageable and your insights more accessible.

Merging and Sorting Data

Merging and sorting data in R are two fundamental operations that significantly enhance your ability to analyze and understand your datasets. Merging allows you to combine data from different sources based on a common identifier, while sorting helps organize your data in a meaningful order, making it easier to spot trends, patterns, and outliers.

Merging Data

The `merge()` function in R is a powerful tool for combining two data frames. It identifies rows in each dataset that have matching values in one or more specified columns and joins these rows together to form a new data frame. The basic syntax of the `merge()` function is as follows:

```r
merged_data <- merge(x, y, by = "ID")
```

In this example, x and y are the data frames you wish to merge, and "ID" is the name of the column you want to merge them by. This column must be present in both data frames. If the column names differ between the two data frames, you can use the `by.x` and `by.y` arguments to specify them separately:

```r
merged_data <- merge(x, y, by.x = "ID_x", by.y = "ID_y")
```

By default, `merge()` performs an inner join, meaning that only rows with matching values in the merge column(s) from both data frames are included in the output. However, you can change the type of join using the `all`, `all.x`, and `all.y` arguments to perform left, right, and outer joins, respectively:

- **Left join** (include all rows from x, and matching rows from y):

r

```r
merged_data <- merge(x, y, by = "ID", all.x = TRUE)
```

- **Right join** (include all rows from y, and matching rows from x):

r

```r
merged_data <- merge(x, y, by = "ID", all.y = TRUE)
```

- **Outer join** (include all rows from both x and y):

r

```r
merged_data <- merge(x, y, by = "ID", all = TRUE)
```

Sorting Data

Sorting your data in R can be achieved using the `order()` function, which returns a permutation that rearranges its first argument into ascending or descending order. To sort a data frame by one or more columns, you can use this function inside square brackets:

r

```r
sorted_data <- my_data_frame[order(my_data_frame$Column), ]
```

This code snippet sorts `my_data_frame` by `Column` in ascending order. To sort in descending order, you can use the – operator before the column name:

r

```r
sorted_data <- my_data_frame[order(-my_data_frame$Column), ]
```

For sorting by multiple columns, you can pass additional arguments to the `order()` function:

```r
sorted_data <- my_data_frame[order(my_data_frame$Column1,
my_data_frame$Column2), ]
```

This will sort `my_data_frame` first by `Column1` and then, within each group of `Column1`, by `Column2`.

The `dplyr` package offers another intuitive way to sort data frames using the `arrange()` function. To sort `my_data_frame` by `Column` in ascending order, you can use:

```r
library(dplyr)
sorted_data <- arrange(my_data_frame, Column)
```

And to sort in descending order, you can use the `desc()` function:

```r
sorted_data <- arrange(my_data_frame, desc(Column))
```

Merging and sorting are crucial steps in preparing your data for analysis. By mastering these operations, you can enhance the quality of your insights and make your data analysis process more efficient and effective. Experiment with these techniques on your datasets to fully grasp their power and flexibility.

CHAPTER 2

Dive into Data Analysis

Importing data into R is a foundational skill for any aspiring data analyst or scientist. The ability to efficiently bring external data into your R environment opens up a world of possibilities for analysis, visualization, and further manipulation. R provides several functions and packages designed to streamline this process, whether your data resides in simple text files, complex Excel spreadsheets, or even on remote databases.

Reading from CSV and Excel Files

CSV files, due to their simplicity and compatibility, are a common format for data storage. R makes it straightforward to import these files using the `read.csv()` function. For example, to load a dataset named `data.csv` into R, you would use the following command:

```R
my_data <- read.csv("path/to/your/data.csv")
```

This function assumes that your CSV file has a header row. If this isn't the case, you can adjust the `header` parameter to `FALSE`.

Excel files, which are more complex due to their potential to hold multiple sheets and more intricate formatting, can be handled using the `readxl` package. After installing and loading `readxl`, you can read a specific sheet from an Excel file with:

```R
library(readxl)
excel_data <- read_excel("path/to/your/file.xlsx", sheet = "Sheet1")
```

Connecting to Databases

For data stored in databases, R can connect to and query these sources directly. The `DBI` package serves as a database interface in R, with many database-specific packages (such as `RMySQL` for MySQL databases, `RSQLite` for SQLite, and `odbc` for ODBC-compliant databases) building on top of `DBI`. Establishing a connection to a database typically involves specifying the database type, server location, database name, username, and password. Once connected, you can use the `dbSendQuery()` function to execute SQL queries and retrieve data directly into R. For instance, connecting to a MySQL database and retrieving data might look like this:

```R
library(DBI)
con <- dbConnect(RMySQL::MySQL(), dbname = "your_database", host = "localhost",
                 user = "your_username", password = "your_password")
query_result <- dbSendQuery(con, "SELECT * FROM your_table")
data <- dbFetch(query_result)
dbClearResult(query_result)
dbDisconnect(con)
```

This process allows for the direct manipulation of database-stored data within the R environment, facilitating a seamless workflow for data analysis and visualization tasks.

Data Cleaning and Preparation

Once data is imported into R, the next critical step is cleaning and preparing it for analysis. Data often comes with inconsistencies, missing values, or irrelevant information that needs to be addressed. The `tidyverse` suite of packages, particularly `dplyr` and `tidyr`, are powerful tools for these tasks.

To handle **missing values**, you can use `na.omit()` to remove any rows with `NA` values, or `replace()` to substitute them with a specific value. For example, to remove all rows with missing data in your dataset:

```R
clean_data <- na.omit(my_data)
```

And to replace all NA values in a specific column with zero:

```R
my_data$column_name[is.na(my_data$column_name)] <- 0
```

Data type conversion is another common necessity. You might need to convert a factor to a numeric type or vice versa. The `as.numeric()`, `as.factor()`, and similar functions are used for these conversions. For instance, converting a character column to numeric:

```R
my_data$numeric_column <- as.numeric(my_data$character_column)
```

Exploratory Data Analysis (EDA) is the process of performing initial investigations on data to discover patterns, spot anomalies, test hypothesis, or check assumptions with the help of summary statistics and graphical representations. It is a crucial step before diving deeper into data modeling or analysis.

To get a summary of your data, including the mean, median, and range of numeric variables, and the frequency of categorical variables, use:

```R
summary(my_data)
```

For a quick look at the distribution of a numeric variable, a histogram is very useful. You can create one with the `ggplot2` package:

```R
library(ggplot2)
ggplot(my_data, aes(x=numeric_column)) + geom_histogram(binwidth = 1)
```

Data Visualization Basics are essential for EDA, allowing you to visually inspect the data for patterns or anomalies that may not be apparent from statistics alone. The `ggplot2` package is a versatile tool for creating a wide range of plots. For example, to create a scatter plot to explore the relationship between two variables:

```R
ggplot(my_data, aes(x=variable1, y=variable2)) + geom_point()
```

These steps of importing, cleaning, preparing, and exploring data are foundational in the data analysis process. Mastering these will enable you to effectively transform raw data into actionable insights.

Importing Data in R

After successfully importing data from CSV and Excel files and establishing connections to databases, it's crucial to delve into the **Data Cleaning and Preparation** phase. This step is indispensable for ensuring the quality and reliability of your data before proceeding with any analysis.

Handling Missing Values is often the first task in data cleaning. Missing data can distort the results of your analysis if not addressed properly. R provides several ways to deal with missing values. The `na.omit()` function is a straightforward approach to exclude any rows with `NA` values from your dataset. However, sometimes you might want to replace missing values with a specific value, such as the mean of the column or a zero. This can be done using the `replace()` function or subsetting with `is.na()`.

R
```
# Removing rows with any NA values
clean_data <- na.omit(my_data)
# Replacing NA values in a specific column with 0
my_data$column_name[is.na(my_data$column_name)] <- 0
```

Data Type Conversion is another critical step in data preparation. It's common to find that some data types are not in the format you need for analysis. For instance, a variable that should be numeric might be interpreted as a character type if it contains non-numeric characters. Converting data types in R is straightforward using functions like `as.numeric()`, `as.character()`, and `as.factor()`.

R
```
# Converting a character column to numeric
my_data$numeric_column <- as.numeric(my_data$character_column)
```

Exploratory Data Analysis (EDA) serves as the bridge between initial data cleaning and deeper analysis. It involves summarizing the main characteristics of a dataset, often with visual methods. A fundamental part of EDA is generating summary statistics, which can be accomplished with the `summary()` function in R. This function provides a quick overview of the central tendencies, dispersion, and shape of your dataset's distribution.

R

```
# Generating summary statistics for your data
summary(my_data)
```

Creating visualizations is another key aspect of EDA, allowing for a more intuitive understanding of the data. The `ggplot2` package offers a powerful and flexible system for creating graphs. For instance, to examine the distribution of a numeric variable, a histogram can be very revealing. Similarly, scatter plots are excellent for exploring the relationship between two quantitative variables.

R

```
# Creating a histogram with ggplot2
library(ggplot2)
ggplot(my_data, aes(x=numeric_column)) + geom_histogram(binwidth = 1)
# Creating a scatter plot to explore relationships between two
variables
ggplot(my_data, aes(x=variable1, y=variable2)) + geom_point()
```

These steps of **importing**, **cleaning**, **preparing**, and **exploring** data are foundational in the data analysis process. By mastering these, you will be well-equipped to transform raw data into insightful conclusions.

Reading from CSV and Excel Files

After successfully importing CSV and Excel files into R, it's essential to understand the nuances of working with these data formats to maximize the efficiency and accuracy of your data analysis. CSV files, being plain text, are straightforward but come with their own set of challenges, such as handling different delimiters, text qualifiers, and missing values. Excel files, on the other hand, introduce complexity with multiple sheets, formatted cells, and potential for non-data elements like images or macros.

When working with CSV files, one common issue is the presence of different delimiters. While the `read.csv()` function assumes a comma as the default separator, many datasets, especially those from European countries, use semicolons or tabs. To address this, R provides the `read.delim()` function for tab-delimited files and the `read.csv2()` function for semicolon-separated files. For example, to read a tab-delimited file, you would use:

R

```
my_data <- read.delim("path/to/your/data.txt")
```

And for a semicolon-separated file:

R

```
my_data <- read.csv2("path/to/your/data.csv")
```

Another challenge is handling text qualifiers. Text fields in CSV files may contain commas, which can disrupt the proper parsing of data. These fields are often enclosed in quotes to differentiate them from actual delimiters. The `read.csv()` function automatically handles fields enclosed in double quotes. However, if your data uses a different qualifier, such as single quotes, you'll need to specify this using the `quote` argument:

R

```
my_data <- read.csv("path/to/your/data.csv", quote = "'")
```

Excel files require attention to sheet names and ranges. Data might not start from the first row or column, and you may need to specify the range of cells to read. The `read_excel()` function from the `readxl` package allows you to define the sheet and the range explicitly. For instance, to read data starting from the second row and first column to the 100th row and 10th column in Sheet1, you would use:

R

```
excel_data <- read_excel("path/to/your/file.xlsx", sheet = "Sheet1", range = "A2:J100")
```

Dealing with missing values is another critical aspect of data preparation. Both CSV and Excel files may contain empty cells representing missing data. By default, R treats these empty cells as NA. However, your dataset might represent missing values differently, such as with a specific marker (e.g., "NA", "NULL", "-"). To correctly identify these values as NA in R, use the na.strings argument:

R

```
my_data <- read.csv("path/to/your/data.csv", na.strings = c("NA",
"NULL", "-"))
```

Lastly, performance can become an issue with very large files. The data.table package offers the fread() function, which is significantly faster than the base R functions for reading text data. It automatically detects the delimiter, handles text qualifiers, and can efficiently manage large datasets:

R

```
library(data.table)
my_data <- fread("path/to/your/data.csv")
```

For Excel files, consider reading only the necessary columns or rows if you're dealing with particularly large files. The read_excel() function allows you to specify columns by name or index, reducing memory usage and speeding up the import process:

R

```
excel_data <- read_excel("path/to/your/file.xlsx", sheet ="Sheet1",
range = "A2:E100", col_types = c("numeric", "text", "text",
"numeric", "date"))
```

By understanding these advanced techniques for reading CSV and Excel files, you can handle a wide range of data import scenarios more effectively. This knowledge ensures that the data you work with is accurately represented in R, setting a solid foundation for any analysis or visualization task ahead.

Connecting to Databases

After establishing a connection to your database using the DBI package and the appropriate driver for your database type, the next step is to interact with the database to perform queries, updates, or deletions. The dbSendQuery() function plays a crucial role in this process. It allows you to send a query to the database and retrieve the result. This function is particularly useful for executing SELECT statements, where you're interested in fetching data based on specific criteria.

Here's a detailed example of how to use `dbSendQuery()` to retrieve data:

```R
# Assuming con is your database connection object
result <- dbSendQuery(con, "SELECT name, age FROM users WHERE age > 21")
# Fetch all matching records
users_over_21 <- dbFetch(result)
# Always clear the result
dbClearResult(result)
```

In this example, `users_over_21` will contain a data frame with the names and ages of users older than 21 years, directly fetched from your database. This method is efficient for handling large datasets because it doesn't load all the data at once. You can control the number of rows fetched by specifying the n parameter in the `dbFetch()` function, which is particularly useful when working with large datasets to avoid memory issues.

For updating or inserting data, you would use `dbSendStatement()` instead. This function is designed for SQL statements that don't return a result set, such as INSERT, UPDATE, DELETE, or even DDL statements like CREATE TABLE. Here's how you might use it to insert a new record:

```R
dbSendStatement(con, "INSERT INTO users (name, age) VALUES ('John Doe', 25)")
```

After executing non-query statements, it's good practice to check the number of affected rows to ensure that your operation was successful. You can do this by using the `dbGetRowsAffected()` function immediately after your `dbSendStatement()` call:

```R
rows_affected <- dbGetRowsAffected(con)
```

For more complex interactions with the database, you might find yourself needing to execute multiple queries or updates as part of a single transaction. R's DBI package supports transactions through the dbBegin(), dbCommit(), and dbRollback() functions. Here's a brief example of how you might use transactions:

```R
dbBegin(con)
dbSendStatement(con, "UPDATE users SET age = age + 1 WHERE name =
'John Doe'")
dbSendStatement(con, "INSERT INTO log (message) VALUES ('Updated
age for John Doe')")
# Commit the transaction
dbCommit(con)
```

In this transaction, both the update and insert operations will be executed as part of a single transaction. If any statement fails, you can roll back the entire transaction to maintain data integrity:

```R
dbBegin(con)
tryCatch({
  dbSendStatement(con, "UPDATE users SET age = age + 1 WHERE name =
'John Doe'")
  dbSendStatement(con, "INSERT INTO log (message) VALUES ('Updated
age for John Doe')")
  dbCommit(con)
}, error = function(e) {
  dbRollback(con)
  message("Transaction failed: ", e$message)
})
```

Transactions are essential for maintaining data consistency, especially when performing multiple related operations that must either all succeed or all fail together.

By mastering these database operations in R, you can efficiently manage and analyze your data directly from your R environment, leveraging the full power of SQL alongside R's analytical capabilities. This seamless integration between R and databases enhances your data analysis workflow, allowing for more sophisticated data manipulation and analysis strategies.

Data Cleaning and Preparation

Once your data is imported into R, the next essential phase is **Data Cleaning and Preparation**. This phase is crucial for ensuring that the data you work with is accurate, consistent, and ready for analysis. The `tidyverse` packages, particularly `dplyr` and `tidyr`, offer a comprehensive set of functions that are instrumental in this process. Let's delve into some of the key steps and techniques involved in cleaning and preparing your data.

Handling Missing Values: Missing data can significantly impact the results of your analysis. Beyond using `na.omit()` and `replace()`, another approach is to impute missing values based on other observations. The `mice` package in R allows for multiple imputation, where missing values are replaced with plausible data points based on the information available. This method is particularly useful in datasets where dropping rows with missing values could lead to a significant loss of data. For example:

```R
library(mice)
imputed_data <- mice(my_data, m=5, method='pmm')
completed_data <- complete(imputed_data, 1)
```

Data Type Conversion: Ensuring that each column in your dataset is of the correct data type is another critical step. Sometimes, numeric values are read as characters, especially if the data comes from a CSV file with numbers that contain commas as thousand separators. The `readr` package provides functions like `parse_number()`, which can correctly interpret such numeric values:

```R
library(readr)
my_data$numeric_column <- parse_number(my_data$character_column)
```

Outlier Detection and Treatment: Outliers can skew your analysis, leading to inaccurate results. Identifying and treating outliers is therefore an important step in data preparation. The `outliers` package offers methods for both detecting and handling outliers. For instance, you can replace outliers with the mean or median of the dataset:

R

```
library(outliers)
outlier_values <- boxplot.stats(my_data$numeric_column)$out
my_data$numeric_column[my_data$numeric_column %in% outlier_values]
<- mean(my_data$numeric_column, na.rm = TRUE)
```

Data Transformation: Transforming data is often necessary to meet the assumptions of statistical tests or improve the effectiveness of machine learning models. The `scale()` function in R can be used to standardize variables, giving them a mean of 0 and a standard deviation of 1. This is particularly useful for algorithms that are sensitive to the scale of the data, such as k-means clustering or logistic regression:

R

```
my_data$standardized_column <- scale(my_data$numeric_column)
```

Creating Dummy Variables: Many statistical models require categorical variables to be converted into a series of binary (0 or 1) variables. This process is known as one-hot encoding. The `fastDummies` package in R simplifies this process, allowing you to quickly convert categorical variables into dummy variables:

R

```
library(fastDummies)
my_data <- dummy_cols(my_data, select_columns = 'categorical_column')
```

Data Aggregation: Aggregating data can be useful when you need to summarize or group your data for analysis. The `dplyr` package provides a straightforward syntax for grouping data and calculating summary statistics. For example, to calculate the average score by group in your dataset:

R

```
library(dplyr)
```

```
grouped_data <- my_data %>%
  group_by(group_column) %>%
  summarise(average_score = mean(score, na.rm = TRUE))
```

Regular Expressions for Data Cleaning: Regular expressions can be powerful tools for cleaning text data. They allow you to search for and replace patterns in your data, such as removing unwanted characters or formatting phone numbers. The `stringr` package in R makes working with regular expressions easier:

R

```
library(stringr)
my_data$text_column <- str_replace_all(my_data$text_column, "[^\\w\
\s]", "")
```

By applying these techniques, you can ensure that your data is clean, consistent, and ready for analysis. Each step in the data cleaning and preparation process is crucial for uncovering accurate and meaningful insights from your data.

Handling Missing Values

Handling missing values in R is a nuanced task that requires a deep understanding of the nature of your data and the implications of various imputation methods. Beyond the basic `na.omit()` and `replace()` functions, there are sophisticated techniques that can help maintain the integrity of your dataset while addressing the gaps caused by missing data. One such approach is conditional imputation, where missing values are filled based on the conditions or relationships within your data. For example, if you're working with a dataset that includes temperature readings from multiple locations and some readings are missing, you might impute these missing values based on the average temperatures of the nearest locations on the same day. This method ensures that the imputed values are realistic and consistent with the dataset's existing patterns.

R

```
library(dplyr)
# Assuming weather_data is your dataset and it contains columns for
location, date, and temperature
weather_data <- weather_data %>%
  group_by(location, date) %>%
```

```
  mutate(temperature = ifelse(is.na(temperature), mean(temperature,
na.rm = TRUE), temperature))
```

Another advanced technique involves using predictive modeling to impute missing values. This method treats the variable with missing values as a dependent variable and uses other variables in the dataset to predict the missing values. The `mice` package, which stands for Multivariate Imputation by Chained Equations, is particularly useful for this purpose. It implements a method that fills in missing data multiple times to create several complete datasets. The variability across these datasets reflects the uncertainty about the right value to impute. After imputation, the analysis is performed on each dataset separately, and the results are pooled to produce estimates and confidence intervals that account for missing data uncertainty.

R

```
library(mice)
# Assuming my_data is your dataset
imputed_data <- mice(my_data, m=5, method='pmm')
completed_data <- complete(imputed_data, 1)
```

When dealing with categorical data, missing values can be particularly challenging. One approach is to add a new category for missing data, which can be useful in analyses where the fact that the data is missing might itself be informative. This method, however, should be used with caution as it introduces additional complexity into the model. In R, this can be done by converting the variable to a factor and adding an extra level for missing values.

R

```
my_data$category_variable <- addNA(my_data$category_variable)
```

For time series data, missing values can disrupt the analysis due to the importance of temporal relationships. Techniques such as linear interpolation or last observation carried forward (LOCF) can be applied to impute missing values in a way that respects the time series nature of the data. The `zoo` package in R provides functions for both of these methods.

```R
R
library(zoo)
# Linear interpolation
my_data$variable <- na.approx(my_data$variable)
# Last observation carried forward
my_data$variable <- na.locf(my_data$variable)
```

It's crucial to remember that the choice of method for handling missing values should be guided by the specific context of your data and the analysis you plan to perform. Each method has its assumptions and implications, and careful consideration is needed to select the most appropriate approach. Additionally, documenting the decisions made during the data cleaning process, including how missing values were handled, is essential for ensuring the transparency and reproducibility of your analysis.

Data Type Conversion

In the realm of data analysis, understanding and executing data type conversion is pivotal for preparing your dataset for accurate and efficient analysis. Data type conversion in R is a straightforward process, but it requires a keen understanding of the types of data you are working with and the goal of your analysis. R provides several functions to convert data types, including `as.numeric()`, `as.character()`, `as.factor()`, and more. These functions are essential tools in your data cleaning and preparation toolkit, allowing you to transform data into the most appropriate format for your analysis needs.

Consider a scenario where your dataset contains a variable that should be numeric, but it was imported as a character string because it contains non-numeric characters or was read from a text file. To perform any mathematical operations on this variable, you first need to convert it to numeric. However, direct conversion using `as.numeric()` on a factor (which might be the case if your character data was automatically converted to a factor by R upon import) will not yield the expected results. Instead, you should first convert the factor to a character string and then to numeric, like so:

```r
r
# Assuming your data frame is named 'df' and the variable is 'var'
df$var <- as.numeric(as.character(df$var))
```

This two-step conversion process ensures that the underlying numeric values represented by the factor levels are correctly converted to numeric type. It's a common pitfall for beginners to overlook this detail, leading to unexpected results in their data analysis.

Another common task is converting numeric data into factors when performing categorical data analysis. Factors in R are used to represent categorical variables and can be ordered or unordered. When dealing with categorical data, it's often necessary to convert numeric IDs or indicators into factors to utilize R's categorical data analysis functions effectively. This conversion can be achieved as follows:

```r
# Converting a numeric variable 'cat_var' into a factor
df$cat_var <- as.factor(df$cat_var)
```

This conversion allows you to leverage R's powerful functions for categorical data, such as `table()`, `xtabs()`, and various modeling functions that treat factors differently from numeric variables.

Data type conversion also plays a crucial role in data visualization. For instance, converting a continuous variable into a categorical variable can simplify the visualization and interpretation of the data. This can be done by creating bins or categories that group the continuous data into discrete intervals:

```r
# Converting a continuous variable 'age' into a categorical
variable 'age_group'
df$age_group <- cut(df$age, breaks = c(0, 18, 35, 65, Inf), labels
= c("Youth", "Young Adult", "Adult", "Senior"))
```

This categorization facilitates the creation of more meaningful visualizations, such as bar plots or pie charts, that compare the counts or proportions of observations within each age group.

In summary, mastering data type conversion in R is essential for effective data cleaning, preparation, and analysis. By understanding how to use R's conversion functions correctly, you can ensure that your data is in the right format to meet the assumptions of statistical tests, leverage R's modeling capabilities fully, and create insightful visualizations. Always remember to inspect your data before and after conversion to verify that the operation has been performed as expected and that no data has been inadvertently altered or lost in the process.

Exploratory Data Analysis (EDA)

Exploratory Data Analysis (EDA) is a critical step in the data analysis process, allowing you to understand the underlying patterns, spot anomalies, test hypotheses, and check assumptions through summary statistics and graphical representations. **R** provides a comprehensive suite of tools for conducting EDA efficiently. One of the first steps in EDA is to use the `summary()` function, which gives you a quick overview of the statistics of each column in your dataset, including mean, median, min, max, and quartiles for numerical data, and frequency counts for categorical data.

```r
summary(your_dataframe)
```

After getting a sense of the data through summary statistics, visualizing the data is your next step. Visualization helps in understanding the distribution, trends, and relationships between variables. **R**'s `ggplot2` package is a powerful tool for creating a wide range of static, dynamic, and interactive visualizations. For instance, to visualize the distribution of a single variable, you can create a histogram using `ggplot2`:

```r
library(ggplot2)
ggplot(your_dataframe, aes(x=your_variable)) +
geom_histogram(binwidth = 1, fill="blue", color="black")
```

Scatter plots are useful for exploring the relationship between two quantitative variables. With `ggplot2`, creating a scatter plot is straightforward:

```r
ggplot(your_dataframe, aes(x=variable1, y=variable2)) +
geom_point()
```

Box plots are another essential tool in EDA for comparing distributions and identifying outliers across different categories:

```r
ggplot(your_dataframe, aes(x=categorical_variable,
y=numeric_variable)) + geom_boxplot()
```

For categorical data, bar charts are useful to visualize the frequency of different categories:

```r
ggplot(your_dataframe, aes(x=factor_variable)) + geom_bar()
```

Correlation analysis is a vital part of EDA when dealing with multiple quantitative variables. The cor() function in R can be used to compute correlation coefficients between pairs of variables, helping to identify potential relationships to investigate further:

```r
cor(your_dataframe$variable1, your_dataframe$variable2)
```

Pairwise plots provide a comprehensive view of all possible bivariate relationships in a dataset and can be easily generated using the pairs() function:

```r
pairs(~variable1 + variable2 + variable3, data = your_dataframe)
```

Finally, for a more interactive exploration of data, packages like plotly and shiny allow you to create dynamic visualizations and web applications directly from R. Interactive plots with plotly can be created as follows:

```r
library(plotly)

plot_ly(data = your_dataframe, x = ~variable1, y = ~variable2, type
= 'scatter', mode = 'markers')
```

These tools and techniques form the backbone of EDA in R, providing a robust framework for understanding and interpreting your data before moving on to more complex analyses or model building. Remember, the goal of EDA is not just to analyze the data but to understand the story it tells and the questions it prompts for further investigation.

Summary Statistics

Building upon the foundation of Exploratory Data Analysis (EDA) and the tools R provides for this purpose, let's delve deeper into summary statistics and how they can be leveraged to extract meaningful insights from your data. Summary statistics are crucial for summarizing the central tendency, dispersion, and shape of a dataset's distribution, among other aspects.

One of the most common measures of central tendency is the mean, which provides an average value of your data. Calculating the mean in R is straightforward using the `mean()` function. However, it's important to note that the mean is sensitive to outliers, which can skew the results. Here's how you can calculate the mean of a numeric variable `var` in a dataframe `df`:

```r
mean_value <- mean(df$var, na.rm = TRUE)
```

The `na.rm = TRUE` argument is crucial as it tells R to ignore NA (missing) values, which are common in real-world datasets and can otherwise lead to errors in your calculations.

Another measure of central tendency is the median, which represents the middle value in your data when it is arranged in ascending order. Unlike the mean, the median is not affected by outliers, making it a more robust measure for skewed distributions. To calculate the median in R, use the `median()` function:

```r
median_value <- median(df$var, na.rm = TRUE)
```

Dispersion in your dataset can be quantified using measures such as variance and standard deviation, which indicate how much the data varies from the mean. The `var()` and `sd()` functions in R calculate the variance and standard deviation, respectively:

```r
variance_value <- var(df$var, na.rm = TRUE)
std_deviation <- sd(df$var, na.rm = TRUE)
```

Understanding the spread of your data is essential, especially when comparing datasets or assessing the variability within your data.

The range of your data, which is the difference between the maximum and minimum values, can be easily found with the `range()` function. However, to get a more detailed view of how your data is spread, the `quantile()` function can be used to calculate quartiles, which divide your data into four equal parts:

r

```r
data_range <- range(df$var, na.rm = TRUE)
quartiles <- quantile(df$var, probs = c(0.25, 0.5, 0.75), na.rm = TRUE)
```

Quartiles are particularly useful for identifying outliers and understanding the distribution of your data beyond the mean or median.

For a quick overview that includes several summary statistics at once, the `summary()` function is incredibly useful. It provides the minimum, maximum, mean, median, and the first and third quartiles for numeric data:

r

```r
summary_stats <- summary(df$var)
```

This function is a powerful tool for initial data exploration, giving you a snapshot of your data's central tendency, dispersion, and shape.

When working with categorical data, frequency counts are a form of summary statistic that shows how often each category appears in the dataset. The `table()` function in R can be used to generate a frequency table:

r

```r
frequency_table <- table(df$categorical_var)
```

This can help in understanding the distribution of categories, identifying the most or least common categories, and spotting any anomalies or errors in your data categorization.

Incorporating these summary statistics into your EDA process provides a solid foundation for understanding your data's structure and characteristics. By applying these techniques, you can uncover insights, inform hypothesis testing, and guide further data analysis and visualization efforts. Remember, the goal of EDA is to make sense of the data you have, and summary statistics are an essential part of that process, offering a concise but comprehensive overview of your dataset's main features.

Data Visualization Basics

Building on the foundation of Exploratory Data Analysis (EDA) and the essential role of summary statistics, we delve deeper into the realm of data visualization in R, focusing on the basics that every aspiring data analyst must master. Visualization is not merely about creating aesthetically pleasing charts and graphs; it's about telling a story with your data, highlighting the key insights, and making complex data more accessible and understandable.

The ggplot2 package, a part of the tidyverse, is a powerful and versatile tool for creating a wide array of data visualizations in R. Its syntax, while initially seeming complex, allows for the creation of highly customizable plots. The package operates on the principle of layering, where you start with a base layer and incrementally add components such as scales, axes, and themes to refine and customize your plot.

To create a basic plot with ggplot2, you start by defining the dataset and mapping the aesthetics (aes), such as x and y axes, color, and size, to your variables. This is followed by adding geometric objects (geom_) that represent the type of plot you want to create, such as points for a scatter plot or bars for a bar chart.

```r
library(ggplot2)
ggplot(data = your_dataframe, aes(x = variable1, y = variable2)) +
  geom_point()
```

This code snippet creates a scatter plot, mapping variable1 to the x-axis and variable2 to the y-axis. The geom_point() function adds a layer of points to the plot, visualizing the relationship between the two variables.

Customization plays a crucial role in enhancing the readability and effectiveness of your plots. `ggplot2` offers numerous options for customization, including adjusting the scales and themes, changing the color and size of geometric objects, and adding labels and titles to make your plots more informative.

For instance, to customize the appearance of the scatter plot and add a title, you can modify the previous example as follows:

```r
ggplot(data = your_dataframe, aes(x = variable1, y = variable2)) +
  geom_point(color = "blue", size = 3) +
  labs(title = "Relationship between Variable 1 and Variable 2",
       x = "Variable 1",
       y = "Variable 2")
```

In this modified version, the points are colored blue, their size is increased for better visibility, and the plot is titled to clearly indicate what it represents. The `labs` function is used to add a main title and label the axes, enhancing the plot's interpretability.

Beyond scatter plots, `ggplot2` enables the creation of a wide variety of plots, including histograms, box plots, and line charts, each suited for different types of data and analysis. For example, to visualize the distribution of a single variable, you might create a histogram:

```r
ggplot(data = your_dataframe, aes(x = variable)) +
  geom_histogram(binwidth = 1, fill = "lightblue", color = "black")
```

This histogram uses `geom_histogram()` to display the distribution of `variable`, with each bin's width set to 1. The fill and color of the bins are customized to improve visual appeal and clarity.

Effective data visualization is a critical skill in data analysis, enabling you to uncover patterns, trends, and outliers that might not be immediately apparent from raw data. By mastering the basics of `ggplot2` and understanding how to leverage its capabilities to create clear, informative, and compelling visualizations, you can significantly enhance your ability to communicate data-driven insights. Whether you're presenting findings to stakeholders, exploring data during the analysis phase, or sharing results with a broader audience, the ability to visualize data effectively is an invaluable asset in your data analysis toolkit.

CHAPTER 3

Mastering Data Visualization

As we delve deeper into the realm of data visualization with **R**, it becomes crucial to understand the concept of **aesthetics** in the **ggplot2** package. Aesthetics are the visual properties of the objects in your graph, such as color, shape, and size. These properties can be mapped to variables in your data, allowing for a more dynamic and informative visualization. For example, mapping the color aesthetic to a categorical variable can help differentiate groups within your data, making the visualization more comprehensible.

```r
ggplot(data = your_dataframe, aes(x = variable1, y = variable2,
color = category_variable)) +
  geom_point()
```

This code snippet demonstrates how to create a scatter plot where points are colored based on a categorical variable, providing an immediate visual distinction between categories.

Another powerful feature of **ggplot2** is the ability to **facilitate comparisons** between groups or over time. Faceting creates multiple plots based on a factor or categorical variable, each showing a subset of the data. This is particularly useful for exploring and presenting the data in a segmented manner, allowing for more targeted analysis and interpretation.

```r
ggplot(data = your_dataframe, aes(x = variable, y = outcome)) +
  geom_line() +
  facet_wrap(~category_variable)
```

In this example, `facet_wrap` is used to generate separate line plots for each level of the `category_variable`, making it easier to compare trends across categories.

The customization of plots in **ggplot2** extends beyond aesthetics and faceting. The package offers various **themes** and **styling options** that can be applied to tailor the appearance of your plots to your specific needs or preferences. Whether you're aiming for a publication-quality figure or a simple plot for exploratory analysis, **ggplot2** provides the tools to adjust text, background, gridlines, and more.

```r
ggplot(data = your_dataframe, aes(x = variable1, y = variable2)) +
  geom_point() +
  theme_minimal() +
  labs(title = "Customized ggplot2 Plot", x = "Variable 1", y =
"Variable 2")
```

By applying the `theme_minimal()` function, this plot adopts a clean and minimalistic style, focusing the viewer's attention on the data itself. The `labs` function is then used to add a custom title and axis labels, enhancing the plot's readability and informative value.

Understanding and utilizing these features of **ggplot2** not only enhances the aesthetic appeal of your visualizations but also their effectiveness in conveying the underlying data story. The ability to customize and control the appearance of your plots is a powerful aspect of **R**'s data visualization capabilities, enabling you to produce insightful and impactful visual representations of your data.

Layering in **ggplot2** goes beyond basic aesthetics and faceting, allowing for the integration of statistical transformations directly within your visualizations. This feature is particularly useful for adding trend lines or performing smoothing operations on your data, which can help highlight underlying patterns or relationships. For instance, adding a linear regression line to a scatter plot can provide insights into the correlation between two variables.

```r
ggplot(data = your_dataframe, aes(x = variable1, y = variable2)) +
  geom_point() +
  geom_smooth(method = "lm", se = FALSE, color = "red")
```

In this code, `geom_smooth` is used with the method set to `"lm"` (linear model) to add a regression line, and `se = FALSE` is specified to remove the shading around the line, which represents the standard error. The color of the line is set to red for better visibility against the points.

Interactivity is another dimension that can significantly enhance the utility and user experience of data visualizations in **R**. Packages such as **plotly** offer the capability to convert static **ggplot2** plots into interactive visualizations with minimal additional coding. This interactivity allows users to hover over data points to see more information, zoom in and out, and even filter data directly within the plot.

```r
library(plotly)
gg <- ggplot(data = your_dataframe, aes(x = variable1, y =
variable2)) +
  geom_point()
ggplotly(gg)
```

By converting a **ggplot2** object with `ggplotly`, the plot becomes interactive, enhancing the exploratory data analysis process by allowing for a more detailed examination of the data points.

The integration of **ggplot2** with **R Markdown** and **Shiny** applications further extends the reach and applicability of your data visualizations. **R Markdown** allows for the creation of dynamic reports that combine code, output, and narrative text, while **Shiny** enables the development of interactive web applications based on **R**. These tools can transform static plots into dynamic visualizations within interactive documents or applications, making your data analysis more accessible and engaging.

Incorporating **ggplot2** visualizations into **Shiny** apps, for example, allows users to interact with the data in real-time, adjusting parameters and filters to see the immediate impact on the visualizations. This dynamic interaction facilitates a deeper understanding and exploration of the data, making **ggplot2** an invaluable tool for both data analysis and presentation.

```r
library(shiny)
ui <- fluidPage(
```

```
  plotOutput("plot")
)
server <- function(input, output) {
  output$plot <- renderPlot({
    ggplot(data = your_dataframe, aes(x = variable1, y =
variable2)) +
      geom_point()
  })
}
shinyApp(ui = ui, server = server)
```

This simple **Shiny** app setup demonstrates how to display a **ggplot2** plot within a web application, offering a template that can be expanded with user inputs and dynamic data filtering.

By mastering these advanced features of **ggplot2** and integrating them with other **R** packages and tools, you can significantly enhance the impact and effectiveness of your data visualizations. Whether through aesthetic customization, statistical layering, interactivity, or dynamic reporting, **ggplot2** provides a comprehensive toolkit for transforming raw data into compelling visual stories.

Introduction to ggplot2

Building upon the foundational knowledge of **ggplot2** and its capabilities in creating dynamic and informative visualizations, it's essential to delve into the more nuanced aspects of this powerful package. One such aspect is the use of **facets** for creating multi-panel plots, which allows for the comparison of different subsets of the data within the same visualization framework. Faceting is particularly useful when you want to explore how relationships between variables might differ across levels of a categorical variable. To implement faceting in **ggplot2**, you can use the `facet_wrap()` or `facet_grid()` functions, depending on whether you want a one-dimensional or two-dimensional layout of panels. Here's how you can create a faceted plot:

```r
ggplot(data = your_dataframe, aes(x = variable1, y = variable2)) +
  geom_point() +
  facet_wrap(~category_variable)
```

This code will generate a series of scatter plots, each corresponding to a different level of `category_variable`, arranged in a single row or column (depending on the size of the plotting area and the number of levels). If you prefer a grid layout, which organizes the panels by two variables, you can use `facet_grid()`:

```r
ggplot(data = your_dataframe, aes(x = variable1, y = variable2)) +
  geom_point() +
  facet_grid(rows_variable ~ cols_variable)
```

In this scenario, `rows_variable` and `cols_variable` determine the arrangement of panels in rows and columns, respectively.

Another critical feature of **ggplot2** is the ability to **customize plot themes**. While the default theme is suitable for exploratory analysis, you might need to adjust your plot's appearance for presentations or publications. **ggplot2** offers several pre-defined themes such as `theme_bw()`, `theme_minimal()`, and `theme_classic()`, among others, which can be applied to any plot to change its overall aesthetics. Additionally, you can use the `theme()` function to customize specific elements of a plot, such as text size, font, and background color. For example, to apply a minimal theme and adjust the title's appearance, you could use:

```r
ggplot(data = your_dataframe, aes(x = variable1, y = variable2)) +
  geom_point() +
  theme_minimal() +
  theme(plot.title = element_text(face = "bold", size = 20))
```

This code applies the `theme_minimal()` to the plot and then customizes the plot title using `theme()`, setting the font to bold and increasing its size.

ggplot2 also excels in creating **complex plots** by layering multiple geometric objects. For instance, you might want to overlay a smooth line on a scatter plot to highlight trends. This can be achieved by adding a `geom_smooth()` layer:

```r
ggplot(data = your_dataframe, aes(x = variable1, y = variable2)) +
  geom_point() +
  geom_smooth(method = "lm", se = TRUE, color = "red")
```

Here, `geom_smooth()` adds a linear model fit to the scatter plot, with `se = TRUE` displaying the confidence interval around the line. The color of the line and its confidence interval is set to red for better visibility.

Lastly, **ggplot2**'s integration with other **R** packages expands its functionality further. For example, the **plotly** package can transform static **ggplot2** plots into interactive web visualizations, and the **gganimate** package can create animations from **ggplot2** plots, useful for showing changes in data over time or illustrating simulation results. These advanced features of **ggplot2** not only enhance the visual appeal of your plots but also make them more informative and engaging for your audience. By mastering these aspects of **ggplot2**, you can leverage the full power of **R**'s data visualization capabilities to tell compelling stories with your data.

Customizing Graphs with ggplot2

Building upon the foundational knowledge of `ggplot2` for creating histograms and scatter plots, let's delve deeper into customizing graphs to make them more informative and visually appealing. Customization is key to making your data visualization stand out and effectively communicate the insights hidden within your data.

Themes and Labels play a crucial role in graph customization. The `theme()` function in `ggplot2` allows for extensive customization of nearly every element of your plot, including background color, grid lines, and text elements. For instance, to remove the background grid and set a minimal theme, you can use:

```R
ggplot(data = your_data, aes(x = your_x_variable, y =
your_y_variable)) +
  geom_point() +
  theme_minimal() +
  theme(panel.grid.major = element_blank(), panel.grid.minor =
element_blank())
```

This code snippet creates a scatter plot with a minimal theme, removing the major and minor grid lines for a cleaner look.

Customizing Text Elements such as titles, axis labels, and legend titles is straightforward with ggplot2. The labs() function is particularly useful for this purpose. You can specify the main title, subtitle, caption, and axis labels within this function. Here's an example:

```R
ggplot(data = your_data, aes(x = your_x_variable, y =
your_y_variable)) +
  geom_point() +
  labs(title = "Your Main Title",
       subtitle = "Your Subtitle",
       caption = "Source: Your Data Source",
       x = "Your X Axis Label",
       y = "Your Y Axis Label")
```

Adjusting Color and Fill for different plot elements can significantly enhance the visual appeal and clarity of your plots. The scale_color_manual() and scale_fill_manual() functions allow you to specify custom colors for different factors in your data. For example, if you're creating a bar plot and want to assign specific colors to different categories, you could use:

```R
ggplot(data = your_data, aes(x = your_factor_variable, fill =
your_category_variable)) +
  geom_bar(stat = "count") +
```

```
  scale_fill_manual(values = c("Category1" = "#1f77b4", "Category2"
= "#ff7f0e"))
```

This code assigns custom colors to each category in your bar plot, making it easier to distinguish between them.

Modifying Plot Dimensions and Aspect Ratio is essential when preparing your visualization for presentations or publications. The `ggsave()` function allows you to save your plot with specific dimensions. For example, to save your plot with a width of 8 inches and a height of 6 inches, you can use:

R
```
ggsave("your_plot_filename.png", plot = last_plot(), width = 8,
height = 6)
```

Remember, the key to effective data visualization in R using `ggplot2` is experimentation and practice. By customizing themes, labels, colors, and dimensions, you can transform basic plots into compelling visual stories that capture your audience's attention and make your insights clear.

Themes and Labels

To further refine the aesthetics of your plots and ensure they communicate the intended message clearly, mastering the use of **themes** and **labels** in `ggplot2` is essential. Beyond the basics, `ggplot2` offers advanced customization options that can significantly enhance the readability and impact of your visualizations.

Fine-tuning Text Elements is crucial for making your plots accessible and understandable. Beyond the basic `labs()` function, `ggplot2` allows for detailed customization of text elements through the `theme()` function. For instance, adjusting the text size, face, and angle of axis text can be done as follows:

R
```
ggplot(data = your_data, aes(x = your_x_variable, y =
your_y_variable)) +
  geom_point() +
  theme(axis.text.x = element_text(size = 12, face = "bold", angle
= 45),
```

```
            axis.text.y = element_text(size = 12, face = "bold", color
= "blue"))
```

This snippet customizes the x-axis text by setting a bold font face, increasing the size, and rotating the text for better fit and readability. Similarly, the y-axis text is made bold and colored blue for emphasis.

Manipulating Plot Background and Grid Lines can dramatically change the look and feel of your plot. If you aim for a clean and modern look, you might want to modify or remove the plot background and grid lines. This can be achieved with:

R

```
ggplot(data = your_data, aes(x = your_x_variable, y =
your_y_variable)) +
   geom_point() +
   theme(plot.background = element_rect(fill = "lightgray"),
         panel.background = element_blank(),
         panel.grid.major = element_line(color = "gray", linetype =
"dashed"),
         panel.grid.minor = element_blank())
```

Here, the plot background is set to a light gray, while the panel background is removed entirely. Major grid lines are customized to be gray and dashed, whereas minor grid lines are removed, creating a clean and uncluttered visual.

Customizing Legends is another aspect where ggplot2 shines, offering control over the position, title, and style of your plot legends. For example, to place the legend at the top of the plot and customize its title and text:

R

```
ggplot(data = your_data, aes(x = your_x_variable, y =
your_y_variable, color = your_factor_variable)) +
   gecm_point() +
   theme(legend.position = "top",
         legend.title = element_text(face = "italic"),
         legend.text = element_text(size = 10))
```

This code moves the legend to the top of the plot and applies italic styling to the legend title while adjusting the legend text size for better legibility.

Adjusting Axis Titles and Plot Title for a cohesive look involves aligning the text style with your plot's overall aesthetic. Consistency in font style, size, and color across your plot titles, axis titles, and labels ensures a professional and polished presentation:

R
```
ggplot(data = your_data, aes(x = your_x_variable, y =
your_y_variable)) +
  geom_point() +
  labs(title = "Plot Title", x = "X Axis Title", y = "Y Axis
Title") +
  theme(plot.title = element_text(size = 20, face = "bold", hjust =
0.5),
        axis.title.x = element_text(size = 14, face = "bold"),
        axis.title.y = element_text(size = 14, face = "bold", color
= "darkred"))
```

In this example, the plot title is bold and centered, while the x-axis title is bold, and the y-axis title is bold and colored dark red, enhancing the visual hierarchy and guiding the viewer's attention effectively.

By leveraging these advanced customization options in ggplot2, you can transform basic plots into insightful and visually appealing stories. The key lies in experimenting with different themes, labels, and styles to find the best fit for your data and the story you wish to tell.

Plot Types

Expanding our exploration of ggplot2 capabilities, we delve into the variety of plot types that can transform raw data into insightful visual narratives. Each plot type serves a unique purpose, catering to different aspects of data analysis and storytelling. Understanding these plot types and their applications is crucial for effective data visualization.

Bar Plots are fundamental for categorical data comparison. They display the counts or aggregate values associated with different categories. Creating a bar plot in ggplot2 is straightforward. For instance, to visualize the count of observations in each category of a factor variable, you can use:

R

```
ggplot(data = your_data, aes(x = your_factor_variable)) +
   geom_bar()
```

This code generates a bar plot with the default count statistic. However, if you're interested in visualizing the sum of another variable for each category, `geom_bar()` can be combined with `stat = "identity"` and `aes(weight = your_numeric_variable)` to achieve this.

Line Plots are ideal for time series data or tracking changes over continuous variables. They highlight trends and patterns over time or ordered categories. To create a line plot, the `geom_line()` function is used:

R

```
ggplot(data = your_data, aes(x = your_time_variable, y =
your_measurement_variable)) +
   geom_line()
```

Adding `group = 1` inside the `aes()` function can be helpful when your data isn't automatically grouped by the plotting function.

Scatter Plots are essential for examining the relationship between two continuous variables. They help identify correlations, trends, and outliers. The `geom_point()` function is used to create scatter plots:

R

```
ggplot(data = your_data, aes(x = your_variable_one, y =
your_variable_two)) +
   geom_point()
```

Customizing scatter plots with colors or shapes based on a third variable adds another dimension to the analysis, enriching the data's story.

Box Plots provide a summary of one or more variables' distribution, highlighting the median, quartiles, and outliers. They are particularly useful for comparing distributions across different categories. To create a box plot, use:

R

```
ggplot(data = your_data, aes(x = your_factor_variable, y =
your_continuous_variable)) +
  geom_boxplot()
```

Histograms are similar to bar plots but are used for continuous data, showing the distribution of a single continuous variable. The `geom_histogram()` function divides the data into bins and counts the number of observations in each bin:

R

```
ggplot(data = your_data, aes(x = your_continuous_variable)) +
  geom_histogram(binwidth = your_preferred_binwidth)
```

Choosing an appropriate `binwidth` is crucial for accurately representing the data's distribution.

Density Plots offer a smooth, continuous estimate of a distribution, which can be more informative than a histogram for understanding the shape of the data's distribution. They are created using `geom_density()`:

R

```
ggplot(data = your_data, aes(x = your_continuous_variable)) +
  geom_density()
```

Violin Plots combine elements of box plots and density plots, showing the distribution's density at different values. They are particularly useful for comparing distributions between groups:

R

```
ggplot(data = your_data, aes(x = your_factor_variable, y =
your_continuous_variable)) +
  geom_violin()
```

Each of these plot types has its strengths and is suited to different types of data and analysis goals. By selecting the appropriate plot type and customizing it to highlight the most relevant aspects of your data, you can reveal the stories hidden within the numbers and communicate them effectively to your audience. Experimentation and practice with these plot types will enhance your data visualization skills, enabling you to present your findings in compelling and informative ways.

Advanced Data Visualization Techniques

Building on the foundation of basic and intermediate visualization techniques, **advanced data visualization** in R allows for more nuanced and sophisticated analysis. This section delves into techniques that leverage the power of R to uncover deeper insights and present data in innovative ways.

Faceting is a technique that enables the creation of multiple related plots within a single figure. It's particularly useful for comparing subsets of data across different categories. The `facet_wrap()` and `facet_grid()` functions in `ggplot2` are instrumental for this purpose. For instance, to create a series of scatter plots for each category in a dataset, you might use:

```R
ggplot(data = your_data, aes(x = variable1, y = variable2)) +
  geom_point() +
  facet_wrap(~category_variable)
```

This code generates a scatter plot for each level of `category_variable`, arranged in a grid that automatically adjusts to the number of categories.

Heatmaps are another advanced visualization tool, ideal for displaying the magnitude of phenomena as colors in two dimensions. They are particularly useful for exploring correlations or patterns in large datasets. Creating a heatmap in R can be achieved with the `geom_tile()` function in `ggplot2`, combined with `scale_fill_gradient()` to customize the color scale:

R

```
ggplot(data = your_data, aes(x = variableX, y = variableY, fill =
value)) +
  geom_tile() +
  scale_fill_gradient(low = "blue", high = "red")
```

This snippet maps `variableX` and `variableY` to the x and y axes, respectively, and uses `value` to determine the color of each tile, with a gradient from blue (low) to red (high).

Interactive Visualizations take data exploration to a new level by allowing users to interact with the visual output. Packages like `plotly` and `shiny` enable the creation of dynamic plots and web applications directly from R. For example, converting a `ggplot2` object to an interactive `plotly` plot is straightforward:

R

```
library(plotly)
gg <- ggplot(data = your_data, aes(x = variable1, y = variable2)) +
geom_point()
ggplotly(gg)
```

This code converts a `ggplot2` scatter plot into an interactive plot that users can zoom, pan, and hover over for more details.

3D Plots offer a way to visualize complex relationships between more than two variables. The `rgl` package in R provides functions for creating interactive 3D plots. A simple 3D scatter plot can be created as follows:

R

```
library(rgl)
with(your_data, plot3d(variable1, variable2, variable3, type = "s",
col = "blue"))
```

This command plots `variable1`, `variable2`, and `variable3` in a 3D space, with points represented as blue spheres.

Network Graphs are essential for visualizing relationships and connections within data, such as social networks or interconnected systems. The `igraph` package in R is a powerful tool for creating and analyzing network graphs. To visualize a simple network:

```R
library(igraph)
g <- graph_from_data_frame(your_data)
plot(g)
```

This code creates a network graph from a dataframe, where each row represents an edge in the network, and plots it.

By mastering these advanced data visualization techniques, you can unlock the full potential of your data, revealing patterns and insights that might not be apparent from traditional plots. Experimentation with these methods will not only enhance your analytical skills but also enable you to communicate complex data stories in compelling and accessible ways.

Interactive Plots with Plotly

Transitioning from static to interactive visualizations marks a significant leap in data analysis and presentation. With `plotly`, a powerful R package, users can create dynamic, interactive plots that enhance the storytelling capabilities of their data. Unlike static graphs, interactive plots allow viewers to engage with the data, exploring details that static visuals can't convey. This section delves into the practical aspects of utilizing `plotly` in R, providing a comprehensive guide to transforming your data visualizations from static to interactive.

To begin with, `plotly` integrates seamlessly with `ggplot2`, enabling a smooth transition from static to interactive visualizations. The process starts by creating a `ggplot2` object, which is then converted into a `plotly` object using the `ggplotly()` function. This conversion retains the aesthetic and mapping of the original `ggplot2` plot, while imbuing it with interactive capabilities such as zooming, panning, and displaying tooltips. Here's a basic example:

```R
library(ggplot2)
```

```r
library(plotly)
# Create a ggplot2 object
p <- ggplot(data = your_data, aes(x = variable1, y = variable2)) +
geom_point()
# Convert to a plotly object
p_interactive <- ggplotly(p)
# Display the interactive plot
p_interactive
```

This code snippet demonstrates the simplicity of transforming a scatter plot into an interactive visualization. The `ggplotly()` function automatically converts the `ggplot2` object, p, into an interactive `plotly` object, `p_interactive`, which can then be displayed in an R environment or embedded in web applications.

Beyond simple conversions, `plotly` offers a rich set of functions for creating interactive plots from scratch. The `plot_ly()` function is at the core of these capabilities, providing a flexible interface for building a wide range of plot types. Here's an example of creating an interactive scatter plot directly using `plot_ly()`:

R

```r
# Create an interactive scatter plot directly with plot_ly
plot_ly(data = your_data, x = ~variable1, y = ~variable2, type =
'scatter', mode = 'markers')
```

In this example, `plot_ly()` is called with the dataset and aesthetic mappings similar to `ggplot2`. The `type` and `mode` arguments specify that the plot is a scatter plot with markers. The tilde (~) before variable names is `plotly`'s syntax for referring to columns in the dataset.

`plotly`'s interactivity is not limited to tooltips and basic navigation. The package allows for the customization of tooltips, enabling the display of additional data on hover. This feature is particularly useful for conveying more complex information without cluttering the visual space. Customizing tooltips involves specifying the `text` argument within `plot_ly()` or adding `hoverinfo` and `hovertemplate` attributes to fine-tune the displayed information:

```R
# Customizing tooltips in an interactive plot
plot_ly(data = your_data, x = ~variable1, y = ~variable2, type =
'scatter', mode = 'markers',
        text = ~paste('Additional Info:',
additional_info_variable), hoverinfo = 'text')
```

This code enhances the scatter plot by displaying a custom tooltip that includes 'Additional Info:' followed by the contents of `additional_info_variable` for each point. The `hoverinfo` argument set to 'text' ensures that only the custom text is displayed when hovering over a marker.

Event handling and dynamic updates are advanced features that `plotly` supports, enabling the creation of truly dynamic data visualizations. These features allow plots to respond to user inputs or changes in the data, making `plotly` a powerful tool for building interactive dashboards and applications within R. While these capabilities require a deeper understanding of `plotly` and possibly integration with `shiny`, they exemplify the potential to create sophisticated data analysis tools that are both informative and engaging.

Incorporating `plotly` into your data visualization toolkit opens up a world of possibilities for data exploration and presentation. By transforming static plots into interactive visualizations, you can provide a more engaging and insightful experience for your audience. Whether you're converting existing `ggplot2` plots or building new interactive visualizations from scratch, `plotly` offers the flexibility and power to bring your data to life. Experimentation with `plotly`'s extensive features will not only enhance your visualizations but also deepen your understanding of the data you're working with.

Creating Dashboards

Dashboards are powerful tools for synthesizing complex data into digestible, interactive, and visually appealing formats. In R, the `shiny` package is a comprehensive solution for building web applications and dashboards directly from R scripts. Dashboards created with `shiny` allow users to interact with your data analysis in real-time, offering a dynamic way to explore datasets and models.

To start creating a dashboard in R, you first need to install and load the `shiny` package. If you haven't already, you can install it using `install.packages("shiny")`, and then load it into your session with `library(shiny)`.

A basic `shiny` app consists of two main components: a user interface (UI) and a server function. The UI defines the layout and appearance of your dashboard, while the server function contains the code to generate the output displayed in the UI. Here's a simple example to illustrate these components:

```R
library(shiny)
# Define UI
ui <- fluidPage(
  titlePanel("My First Shiny Dashboard"),
  sidebarLayout(
    sidebarPanel(
      sliderInput("num",
                  "Choose a number:",
                  min = 1,
                  max = 100,
                  value = 50)
    ),
    mainPanel(
      textOutput("result")
    )
  )
)
# Define server logic
server <- function(input, output) {
  output$result <- renderText({
    paste("You selected", input$num)
  })
}
# Run the application
shinyApp(ui = ui, server = server)
```

In this example, `fluidPage` is used to create a fluid and responsive layout that adjusts to the size of the user's screen. `titlePanel` adds a title to the dashboard, and `sidebarLayout` divides the UI into a sidebar and main panel. The `sliderInput` function creates a slider in the sidebar, allowing users to select a number between 1 and 100. The `mainPanel` displays the output, which, in this case, is the number selected by the user, shown through `textOutput`.

The server function listens for changes in the input (the slider position) and updates the output accordingly. The `renderText` function generates a text output that concatenates "You selected" with the current value of the slider (`input$num`).

To enhance your dashboard, `shiny` offers various functions to customize the UI with different input controls like checkboxes, radio buttons, and dropdown menus, as well as output elements including plots, tables, and HTML content. The `plotOutput` function, for example, can display plots generated with `ggplot2` or base R graphics, making it straightforward to incorporate sophisticated data visualizations into your dashboard.

For more complex dashboards, `shiny` modules can be used to organize code into reusable pieces. Modules help in managing larger applications by allowing you to isolate UI and server code for specific tasks into separate, reusable units.

Additionally, `shinydashboard` is an extension package that provides functions to create dashboards with a standard dashboard appearance, including headers, sidebars, and body content areas. This package can be particularly useful for creating dashboards that follow a traditional layout pattern, offering a set of predefined UI components that are commonly used in dashboards.

To further customize the appearance and functionality of your dashboard, CSS and JavaScript can be integrated into `shiny` applications. This allows for detailed styling and interactive behaviors beyond what is available through R code alone.

By leveraging the `shiny` package, you can transform your R analyses into interactive dashboards, making your data more accessible and engaging for users. Whether for exploratory data analysis, presenting results to stakeholders, or creating interactive tools for data-driven decision-making, `shiny` dashboards offer a versatile platform for data visualization and application development in R.

CHAPTER 4

Data Transformation and Analysis

In this chapter, we delve into the transformative power of the `dplyr` package for data transformation and analysis in R. `dplyr` is a cornerstone for any data scientist working with R, offering a coherent set of verbs that help in simplifying data manipulation tasks. The package's syntax is both intuitive and expressive, making it an indispensable tool for both beginners and seasoned analysts. To start, let's focus on two fundamental operations: selecting and filtering data.

Selecting Data with `dplyr`

The `select()` function in `dplyr` allows you to choose a subset of columns from a dataset. This is particularly useful when working with wide datasets containing numerous variables, but you are only interested in a few. The basic syntax of `select()` is straightforward:

```r
library(dplyr)
selected_data <- select(dataset, column1, column2, column3)
```

This code snippet demonstrates how to select `column1`, `column2`, and `column3` from `dataset`. `dplyr` also provides a variety of helper functions like `starts_with()`, `ends_with()`, `contains()`, `matches()`, and `everything()` which can be used within `select()` to efficiently specify the columns you want to work with.

Filtering Data with `dplyr`

Filtering rows based on conditions is another core task in data analysis. The `filter()` function in `dplyr` makes this task intuitive. You can specify one or more conditions that rows must meet to be included in the output. Here's a simple example:

```r
filtered_data <- filter(dataset, condition1, condition2)
```

In this example, `dataset` is filtered to include only rows that meet `condition1` and `condition2`. Conditions are written using the column names directly, making the code both readable and concise. Logical operators such as `&` (and), `|` (or), and `!` (not) can be used to combine or negate conditions.

Both `select()` and `filter()` are part of `dplyr`'s core set of data manipulation verbs, which also include `mutate()`, `summarize()`, `arrange()`, and more. These functions are designed to work seamlessly with the `%>%` operator (pronounced as pipe operator), which allows for the chaining of multiple data manipulation steps in a clear and readable manner. For instance:

```r
dataset %>%
  select(column1, column2) %>%
  filter(condition1) %>%
  arrange(column1)
```

This code snippet demonstrates a typical data manipulation workflow where a dataset is first trimmed down to only two columns, then filtered by a condition, and finally arranged in ascending order based on `column1`. The use of the pipe operator `%>%` facilitates understanding the sequence of operations and editing or extending the workflow as needed.

As we continue to explore the capabilities of `dplyr`, it's important to practice these operations with real datasets to fully grasp their power and flexibility. In the following sections, we will delve deeper into summarizing data, which is another critical aspect of data analysis that `dplyr` simplifies significantly.

Summarizing Data with `dplyr`

The `summarize()` function in `dplyr` is a powerful tool for reducing datasets to essential summaries, making it easier to understand the underlying patterns and trends. By applying various aggregation functions, you can compute summary statistics such as mean, median, sum, and count. Here's how you can use `summarize()` to calculate the average value of a column:

```r
summary_data <- dataset %>%
  group_by(grouping_column) %>%
  summarize(average_value = mean(target_column, na.rm = TRUE))
```

In this example, `dataset` is first grouped by `grouping_column` using the `group_by()` function. Then, `summarize()` calculates the mean of `target_column`, excluding missing values with `na.rm = TRUE`. This pattern is particularly useful for understanding differences across groups or categories within your data.

Tidying Data with `tidyr`

While `dplyr` focuses on manipulating your data, `tidyr` complements these efforts by tidying your data. Tidy data means each variable forms a column, each observation forms a row, and each type of observational unit forms a table. The `pivot_longer()` and `pivot_wider()` functions are central to changing the shape of your tables to meet this standard. For instance, converting data from wide to long format can be achieved as follows:

```r
long_data <- pivot_longer(data = wide_data, cols =
starts_with("year"), names_to = "year", values_to = "value")
```

This transformation is crucial for making data analysis and visualization tasks more straightforward, as many of R's functions are designed to work best with data in a tidy format.

Joining and Binding Data Frames

Merging datasets is a common task in data analysis. `dplyr` offers several functions to join data frames by matching on one or more keys. The `left_join()`, `right_join()`, `inner_join()`, and `full_join()` functions allow you to combine data frames in different ways depending on your specific needs. Here's an example of a left join:

```r
merged_data <- left_join(data1, data2, by = "key_column")
```

This code merges `data1` and `data2` by matching rows based on `key_column`, keeping all rows from `data1` and adding matching rows from `data2`. If there are no matches, the result will have `NA` in the columns from `data2`.

Date and Time Data Handling

Working with date and time data is another area where R excels, thanks to packages like `lubridate`. Handling dates and times efficiently can be challenging, but `lubridate` simplifies this process. For example, parsing a date string into a date object can be done as follows:

```r
library(lubridate)
date_object <- ymd("20230101")
```

This function converts a character string in the format "yearmonthday" into a Date object, making it easier to perform operations like calculating differences between dates or extracting components like the month or day of the week.

By mastering these data transformation and analysis techniques in R, you'll be well-equipped to tackle a wide range of data science challenges. The key is to practice these skills on real datasets, allowing you to apply what you've learned and gain confidence in your ability to manipulate and analyze data effectively.

The dplyr Package

The `mutate()` function in `dplyr` is a versatile tool for adding new columns to your dataset or transforming existing ones. It allows you to perform operations on your data frame, such as calculations across columns or row-wise transformations. For example, if you want to create a new column that is the sum of two existing columns, you can use `mutate()` as follows:

```r
transformed_data <- dataset %>%
  mutate(new_column = column1 + column2)
```

This code snippet adds a new column named `new_column` to `dataset`, where each row in `new_column` is the sum of the corresponding rows in `column1` and `column2`. The beauty of `mutate()` lies in its ability to handle various types of operations, including mathematical calculations, logical operations, and even complex custom functions.

Another powerful feature of `dplyr` is the `summarize()` function, which allows you to generate summary statistics of different variables in your data frame. When combined with `group_by()`, `summarize()` becomes even more powerful, enabling you to calculate summaries for groups of data. For instance, to calculate the average of a column for each group defined by another column, you can use:

```r
summary_data <- dataset %>%
  group_by(group_column) %>%
  summarize(average_value = mean(target_column, na.rm = TRUE))
```

In this example, `dataset` is first grouped by `group_column`, and then the mean of `target_column` is calculated for each group, excluding any missing values with `na.rm = TRUE`. This pattern is incredibly useful for exploring your data and understanding the relationships between different variables.

The `arrange()` function in `dplyr` is used to sort your data frame by one or more columns. You can specify ascending or descending order for each column. For example, to sort your dataset in ascending order of `column1` and then in descending order of `column2`, you can write:

r
```r
sorted_data <- dataset %>%
  arrange(column1, desc(column2))
```

This code will first sort `dataset` in ascending order based on `column1`. For rows with the same value in `column1`, it will then sort in descending order based on `column2`. Sorting is a fundamental step in data analysis, as it can help you quickly identify patterns, outliers, or anomalies in your data.

`dplyr` also provides functions for joining different datasets together based on common keys. The `left_join()` function, for example, will merge two data frames by matching rows from the first data frame with rows from the second data frame based on one or more key columns. If there are rows in the first data frame that do not have matching rows in the second data frame, those rows will still be included in the result with `NA` in the columns from the second data frame. Here's how you can use `left_join()`:

r
```r
joined_data <- left_join(data1, data2, by = "key_column")
```

This code snippet merges `data1` and `data2` by matching rows based on `key_column`, keeping all rows from `data1` and adding matching rows from `data2`. Joining data frames is a common task when you need to combine data from multiple sources for comprehensive analysis.

By leveraging these `dplyr` functions, you can perform a wide range of data manipulation tasks more efficiently. The key to mastering `dplyr` is practice. Try applying these functions to real datasets and explore the various options and arguments each function offers. This hands-on experience will deepen your understanding of data manipulation in R and enhance your data analysis skills.

Selecting and Filtering Data

The `dplyr` package in R simplifies data manipulation, making it easier to select and filter data based on specific criteria. After understanding the basics of selecting columns and filtering rows, we can further explore the capabilities of `dplyr` to refine our data analysis process.

Combining `select()` and `filter()` for Efficient Data Manipulation

Combining `select()` and `filter()` functions can streamline data manipulation tasks. For instance, if you need to work with a subset of columns and also want to apply certain conditions to filter rows, you can chain these functions together using the pipe operator `%>%`. Here's an example:

```r
library(dplyr)
# Selecting specific columns and filtering rows
dataset %>%
  select(column1, column2, column3) %>%
  filter(condition1, condition2)
```

This approach allows you to succinctly specify the columns of interest and the conditions for filtering, making your code more readable and easier to maintain.

Using `slice()` for Row Selection

Another useful function in `dplyr` for data selection is `slice()`. This function selects rows by their position. It is particularly handy when you want to retrieve the top or bottom n rows after arranging your dataset. For example, to select the first 10 rows of a dataset, you can use:

```r
top_ten_rows <- dataset %>%
  arrange(column1) %>%
  slice(1:10)
```

Advanced Filtering with `filter()` and Logical Operators

`dplyr`'s `filter()` function becomes even more powerful when combined with logical operators. You can use `&` for "and", `|` for "or", and `!` for "not" to create complex filtering conditions. For example, to filter a dataset for rows where `column1` is greater than 10 and `column2` is not equal to 'value', you can write:

```r
dataset %>%
  filter(column1 > 10 & column2 != 'value')
```

Dealing with Missing Values

When working with real-world data, missing values are common. `dplyr` provides a straightforward way to filter out rows with missing values using the `na.omit()` function. Alternatively, within the `filter()` function, you can use `is.na()` to filter rows based on the presence or absence of NA values. For example, to keep rows where `column1` does not have missing values:

```r
dataset %>%
  filter(!is.na(column1))
```

Dynamic Column Selection with `select()` Helpers

`dplyr` offers several helper functions within `select()` to dynamically choose columns based on certain criteria. Functions like `starts_with()`, `ends_with()`, `contains()`, and `matches()` can be used to select columns without explicitly naming them. This is particularly useful for datasets with a large number of columns. For instance, to select all columns that start with "prefix_":

```r
dataset %>%
  select(starts_with("prefix_"))
```

Summarizing Filtered Data

After filtering your data, you might want to summarize it to extract insights. `dplyr`'s `summarize()` function can be used in conjunction with `group_by()` to calculate summary statistics for subsets of your data. For example, to calculate the average of `column1` for each group defined by `group_column`:

```r
dataset %>%
  filter(condition) %>%
  group_by(group_column) %>%
  summarize(average_column1 = mean(column1, na.rm = TRUE))
```

This code filters the dataset based on a condition, groups the remaining data by group_column, and then calculates the mean of column1 for each group, handling missing values by excluding them from the calculation.

By mastering the selection and filtering capabilities of dplyr, you can efficiently manipulate and analyze your data. Practice applying these techniques to various datasets to become proficient in data transformation and analysis with R.

Summarizing Data

The summarize() function in dplyr is instrumental in condensing large datasets into meaningful summaries, providing insights that are essential for data analysis. This function works seamlessly with group_by() to offer a granular look at data, allowing for the computation of various summary statistics within each group. For example, to understand the distribution of a dataset, you might be interested in calculating the minimum, maximum, mean, and standard deviation of a particular variable. The following code snippet demonstrates how to achieve this:

```r
library(dplyr)
# Calculating summary statistics for a specific column
summary_stats <- dataset %>%
  group_by(group_column) %>%
  summarize(
    min_value = min(target_column, na.rm = TRUE),
    max_value = max(target_column, na.rm = TRUE),
    mean_value = mean(target_column, na.rm = TRUE),
    sd_value = sd(target_column, na.rm = TRUE)
  )
```

In this example, dataset is first grouped by group_column. Then, for each group, the minimum, maximum, mean, and standard deviation of target_column are calculated, with na.rm = TRUE ensuring that missing values are ignored in these calculations. This approach is particularly useful when you need to compare these statistics across different groups or categories within your data.

Beyond basic summary statistics, dplyr also enables the computation of more complex aggregations. For instance, you might want to count the number of observations that meet a certain criterion within each group. This can be accomplished by combining summarize() with conditional statements inside sum():

```r
# Counting observations that meet a specific condition within each
group
condition_counts <- dataset %>%
   group_by(group_column) %>%
   summarize(count_condition = sum(target_column > threshold, na.rm
= TRUE))
```

Here, dataset is grouped by group_column, and within each group, summarize() counts the number of times target_column exceeds a specified threshold. The na.rm = TRUE parameter ensures that missing values do not interfere with the count.

Another powerful feature of dplyr is its ability to handle multiple summary operations in a single call to summarize(), making it possible to perform a comprehensive analysis of your data with minimal code. For example, to calculate the mean, median, and the number of unique values in a column, you can use:

```r
# Performing multiple summary operations
multi_summary <- dataset %>%
   group_by(group_column) %>%
   summarize(
     mean_value = mean(target_column, na.rm = TRUE),
     median_value = median(target_column, na.rm = TRUE),
     n_unique = n_distinct(target_column)
   )
```

This code snippet demonstrates the versatility of `summarize()` in `dplyr`, allowing for the calculation of mean, median, and the count of unique values in `target_column` for each group defined by `group_column`. Such detailed summarization is invaluable for gaining a deeper understanding of the data's structure and underlying patterns.

To further enhance the utility of summarized data, `dplyr` can be integrated with other packages for visualization, such as `ggplot2`, enabling the creation of compelling visual summaries that can reveal trends and insights at a glance. For instance, after summarizing your data, you might want to visualize the average values of a variable across groups:

```r
library(ggplot2)
# Visualizing summary statistics
ggplot(summary_stats, aes(x = group_column, y = mean_value)) +
  geom_col() +
  labs(title = "Average Values by Group", x = "Group", y = "Average
Value")
```

This example illustrates how summarized data can be directly fed into `ggplot2` to produce a bar chart displaying the average values of `target_column` across different groups. Visual summaries like this are crucial for communicating findings and supporting decision-making processes.

By mastering the summarization capabilities of `dplyr`, you can efficiently extract meaningful insights from your data, paving the way for advanced analysis and visualization. The key to leveraging these capabilities is practice and experimentation with real datasets, allowing you to explore the full spectrum of summarization techniques and their applications in data science.

Tidying Data with tidyr

The `tidyr` package in R is designed to help you transform your data into a tidy format, where each column is a variable, each row is an observation, and each table is a type of observational unit. This structure makes it easier to work with your data, especially when applying various data manipulation and analysis functions. Let's delve into some of the key functions provided by `tidyr` for tidying data.

Pivoting Data

Data often comes in a wide format, where you have multiple columns for what essentially represents the same variable. For example, you might have a dataset with columns for each year (`year_2020`, `year_2021`, etc.), which would be better represented as two columns: one for the year and one for the value. `tidyr` provides two main functions to pivot data: `pivot_longer()` and `pivot_wider()`.

- **Using** `pivot_longer()`

To convert data from a wide format to a long format, you use `pivot_longer()`. This is particularly useful when you have multiple columns that should be a single variable.

```r
long_data <- pivot_longer(
  data = wide_data,
  cols = starts_with("year"),
  names_to = "year",
  values_to = "value"
)
```

In this example, all columns that start with "year" are collapsed into two columns: `year` and `value`, where `year` contains the year and `value` contains the data associated with that year.

- **Using** `pivot_wider()`

Conversely, you might encounter situations where your data is in a long format but would be more useful in a wide format. For this, `pivot_wider()` is the function to use.

```r
wide_data <- pivot_wider(
  data = long_data,
  names_from = year,
  values_from = value
)
```

This code takes `long_data`, which has a `year` column and a `value` column, and spreads it into a wide format, creating a new column for each unique value in the `year` column.

Separating and Uniting Columns

Sometimes, a single column contains two or more pieces of information. For example, a `date_time` column might contain both the date and the time, which you might want to analyze separately.

- **Using** `separate()`

The `separate()` function splits a column into multiple columns.

```r
separated_data <- separate(
  data = combined_data,
  col = date_time,
  into = c("date", "time"),
  sep = " "
)
```

This code splits the `date_time` column into two columns, `date` and `time`, using a space as the separator.

- **Using** `unite()`

If you need to do the opposite and combine two columns into one, you can use the `unite()` function.

```r
united_data <- unite(
  data = separated_data,
  col = date_time,
  c("date", "time"),
  sep = " "
)
```

Here, the `date` and `time` columns are combined back into a single `date_time` column, with a space separating the original values.

Handling Missing Values

When tidying data, you might also need to address missing values. `tidyr` offers the `drop_na()` function, which removes rows with missing values in specified columns.

```r
clean_data <- drop_na(
  data = messy_data,
  c(col1, col2)
)
```

This code removes any rows from `messy_data` where `col1` or `col2` have missing values.

Nesting and Unnesting Data

For more complex data structures, `tidyr` provides functions for nesting and unnesting data frames. Nesting allows you to create a list-column of data frames, which can be useful for modeling.

- **Using** `nest()`

```r
nested_data <- nest(
  data = wide_data,
  cols = c(col1, col2)
)
```

This creates a new data frame where `col1` and `col2` are nested into a single list-column.

- **Using** `unnest()`

To reverse the process, you can use `unnest()`.

```r
unnested_data <- unnest(
  data = nested_data,
  col = nested
)
```

This code takes the nested list-column and expands it back into the original columns.

By mastering these `tidyr` functions, you can efficiently transform your data into a tidy format, making it more accessible and easier to analyze with tools like `ggplot2` and `dplyr`. Practice with real datasets to become proficient in tidying data and unlocking the full potential of your data analysis in R.

Joining and Binding Data Frames

In addition to the `left_join()` function, `dplyr` provides several other types of joins to cater to different merging scenarios. Each of these functions requires at least two data frames and a common key (or keys) to match the rows. Understanding the nuances of each join type is crucial for effective data manipulation.

- `right_join(data1, data2, by = "key_column")`: This function works similarly to `left_join()` but keeps all rows from `data2` and adds matching rows from `data1`. If there are no matches in `data1`, the result will have `NA` in the columns from `data1`.

- `inner_join(data1, data2, by = "key_column")`: An `inner_join()` returns only the rows that have matching values in both data frames. This is useful when you only want to keep observations that are present in both datasets.

- `full_join(data1, data2, by = "key_column")`: This function combines `left_join()` and `right_join()`, keeping all rows from both `data1` and `data2`. Where there are no matches, you will see `NA` in the respective columns.

- `semi_join(data1, data2, by = "key_column")`: Unlike the other joins, a `semi_join()` returns all rows from `data1` that have a match in `data2`. However, it does not add any columns from `data2` to the result. This is particularly useful for filtering rows in one data frame based on their presence in another.

- `anti_join(data1, data2, by = "key_column")`: The opposite of a `semi_join()`, an `anti_join()` returns all rows from `data1` that do not have a match in `data2`, effectively filtering out the rows that are present in both datasets.

For scenarios where you need to combine rows from two datasets rather than columns, `dplyr` offers two binding functions:

- `bind_rows(data1, data2)`: This function stacks `data2` below `data1`, effectively appending the rows of `data2` to `data1`. It's important that both data frames have the same columns for `bind_rows()` to work properly. If there are columns that do not match, `NA` values will be inserted in the missing spots.

- `bind_cols(data1, data2)`: Conversely, `bind_cols()` adds the columns of `data2` to `data1`, side by side. This requires that both data frames have the same number of rows. If the row counts differ, an error will be thrown.

When working with these functions, it's essential to ensure that the data types of the key columns match across the data frames being joined or bound. Mismatches in data types can lead to unexpected results or errors. Additionally, when using `bind_rows()`, be mindful of the fact that column names need to match for the rows to align correctly. If the column names differ, you might end up with a data frame that has more columns than intended, filled with `NA` values where the names did not align.

Here's an example of how to use `full_join()` to merge two datasets:

```r
# Assuming data1 and data2 share a common key column named 'id'
merged_data <- full_join(data1, data2, by = "id")
```

This code snippet will merge `data1` and `data2` on the `id` column, keeping all rows from both data frames. Where `id` values match, the rows will be combined into a single row in the output; where they do not, the output will contain rows from each data frame with `NA` in the columns that lacked a match.

By mastering these joining and binding functions, you can manipulate and combine datasets in R with precision, enabling more complex and comprehensive data analysis tasks.

Date and Time Data Handling

Handling date and time data in R is crucial for many data analysis tasks, as it allows you to perform time-based calculations, comparisons, and aggregations. The `lubridate` package in R simplifies the work with dates and times. Here, we'll delve into some advanced functionalities of `lubridate` and how to use them effectively.

Working with Time Zones

Time zones can significantly impact your data analysis, especially when dealing with global data. `lubridate` provides functions to easily convert between time zones. The `with_tz()` function allows you to change the time zone of a date-time object without altering the actual time.

```r
library(lubridate)
date_time <- ymd_hms("2023-01-01 12:00:00", tz = "UTC")
date_time_ny <- with_tz(date_time, "America/New_York")
```

Rounding Dates and Times

Rounding off date and time objects can simplify your analysis by grouping data into more manageable intervals. `lubridate` offers functions like `floor_date()`, `ceiling_date()`, and `round_date()` to round down, up, or to the nearest unit of time, respectively.

```r
rounded_down <- floor_date(date_time, "day")
rounded_up <- ceiling_date(date_time, "month")
rounded_nearest <- round_date(date_time, "hour")
```

Durations, Periods, and Intervals

Understanding the difference between durations, periods, and intervals is key to accurately manipulating and calculating with date-time objects. Durations measure time spans in exact seconds, periods account for variable lengths (like months, years), and intervals represent time spans between two points.

- **Durations**: Use `durations()` for precise time spans that don't consider calendar specifics.

- **Periods**: Use `periods()` when you need to consider months, years, and daylight savings time.

- **Intervals**: Use `intervals()` to work with specific start and end dates.

r
```
duration_example <- as.duration(days(5))
period_example <- months(1) + days(5)
interval_example <- interval(start = ymd("2023-01-01"), end = ymd("2023-02-01"))
```

Dealing with Daylight Savings Time

Daylight savings time (DST) can introduce unexpected behavior in time series data. `lubridate` helps manage DST transitions smoothly. When performing operations across a DST change, `lubridate` automatically adjusts for the time shift.

r
```
dst_transition <- ymd_hms("2023-03-14 02:00:00", tz = "America/New_York")
dst_adjusted <- dst_transition + days(1)
```

Sequences of Dates and Times

Generating sequences of dates or times is a common task, for instance, when creating time series data from scratch. The `seq()` function from base R, combined with `lubridate`'s date-time functions, can generate regular sequences.

r
```
date_seq <- seq(ymd("2023-01-01"), by = "month", length.out = 12)
```

Extracting and Modifying Components of Date-Time Objects

`lubridate` makes it easy to extract or modify components of a date-time object, such as years, months, days, or hours. This is particularly useful for feature engineering in machine learning models.

r
```
year_component <- year(date_time)
month_component <- month(date_time)
day_component <- day(date_time)
hour_component <- hour(date_time)
```

```
# Modifying components
updated_date_time <- update(date_time, year = 2024, month = 12)
```

By mastering these `lubridate` functionalities, you can handle a wide range of date and time data manipulation tasks in R, from basic transformations to complex time zone conversions and DST adjustments. This knowledge will significantly enhance your data analysis and visualization capabilities in R, allowing you to uncover deeper insights from temporal data.

CHAPTER 5

Statistical Analysis in R

Statistical analysis in R begins with understanding the **basic statistical concepts** that underpin most analytical methods. One of the first steps in any statistical analysis is to describe and summarize the dataset you're working with. R provides a comprehensive suite of functions for calculating **summary statistics**, which give you a snapshot of your data's central tendency, dispersion, and shape.

To start, the `summary()` function in R can be used to quickly obtain a summary of each variable in your dataset. For a numeric variable, this typically includes the minimum, maximum, mean, median, and quartiles. For example:

```r
data_summary <- summary(your_dataframe)
print(data_summary)
```

Understanding the distribution of your data is crucial before you proceed with any further analysis. The `mean()` and `median()` functions can be used to find the central tendency of your data, while `sd()` calculates the standard deviation, providing insight into the variability of your dataset.

```r
data_mean <- mean(your_dataframe$your_variable)
data_median <- median(your_dataframe$your_variable)
data_sd <- sd(your_dataframe$your_variable)
```

For a more visual exploration of your data, R's base plotting functions or the `ggplot2` package can be used to create histograms, box plots, or density plots. These visualizations can help identify outliers, skewness, and the overall distribution shape, which are important factors to consider before applying statistical tests or models.

r

```
hist(your_dataframe$your_variable, main = "Histogram of Your
Variable", xlab = "Your Variable")
```

After exploring the basic characteristics of your data, the next step often involves hypothesis testing to make inferences about your population based on your sample data. R supports a wide range of hypothesis tests, including t-tests, ANOVA, and chi-squared tests, each applicable under different conditions and assumptions about your data. For instance, to compare the means of two independent samples, you might use the `t.test()` function:

r

```
t_test_result <- t.test(sample1, sample2)
print(t_test_result)
```

It's essential to understand the assumptions underlying each statistical test, such as normality and homogeneity of variances, as violating these assumptions can lead to incorrect conclusions. Tools like the `shapiro.test()` for testing normality and `var.test()` for comparing variances can help verify these assumptions.

As you delve deeper into statistical analysis in R, you'll encounter more complex techniques and models, including linear regression analysis, which allows you to explore relationships between variables. The `lm()` function in R facilitates the fitting of linear models, enabling you to not only understand these relationships but also make predictions based on your data.

r

```
linear_model <- lm(dependent_variable ~ independent_variable, data
= your_dataframe)
summary(linear_model)
```

Linear regression analysis is a powerful tool for data analysis, offering insights into the factors that influence your dependent variable. However, it's important to check the model diagnostics to ensure that your model meets the necessary assumptions, such as linearity, independence of errors, homoscedasticity, and normality of residuals.

For assessing the quality of your linear model, diagnostic plots play a crucial role. The `plot()` function can be applied to a model object in R, providing valuable visuals such as Residuals vs Fitted, Normal Q-Q, Scale-Location, and Residuals vs Leverage plots. These plots help in identifying potential problems like non-linearity, heteroscedasticity, outliers, and leverage points.

```r
plot(linear_model)
```

Beyond linear regression, R offers capabilities for conducting logistic regression, which is used when the dependent variable is categorical. The `glm()` function is used for fitting generalized linear models, including logistic regression. For example, to model a binary outcome based on one or more predictors, you might use:

```r
logistic_model <- glm(dependent_variable ~ independent_variable,
family = binomial, data = your_dataframe)
summary(logistic_model)
```

Logistic regression analysis provides odds ratios, confidence intervals, and significance levels, which are essential for understanding the relationship between the dependent and independent variables in cases where the outcome is binary.

When moving towards more advanced statistical modeling, R supports techniques such as ANOVA for comparing means across multiple groups. The `anova()` function can be used to analyze the differences among group means and to determine if any of those differences are statistically significant.

```r
anova_model <- aov(dependent_variable ~ independent_variable, data
= your_dataframe)
summary(anova_model)
```

For categorical data analysis, the Chi-squared test is a common choice. It allows you to test the independence between two categorical variables. The `chisq.test()` function in R makes it straightforward to perform this test.

```r
chi_squared_test_result <-
chisq.test(table(your_dataframe$variable1,
your_dataframe$variable2))
print(chi_squared_test_result)
```

As you progress in your statistical analysis journey, you might also explore non-parametric tests, which are useful when your data do not meet the assumptions required by parametric tests. Functions such as `wilcox.test()` for the Wilcoxon rank-sum test and `kruskal.test()` for the Kruskal-Wallis test expand your analytical capabilities in R.

```r
wilcox_test_result <- wilcox.test(sample1, sample2)
kruskal_test_result <- kruskal.test(list(sample1, sample2,
sample3))
```

Each of these statistical methods and tests opens up new avenues for data analysis, allowing you to extract meaningful insights from your data. Whether you are comparing groups, exploring relationships, or making predictions, R provides a comprehensive toolkit for statistical analysis. By leveraging these tools and techniques, you can uncover the stories hidden within your data, guiding decision-making processes and contributing to knowledge in your field of study or work.

Basic Statistical Concepts

Understanding **correlation** is fundamental in statistical analysis as it helps in determining the relationship between two variables. In R, the `cor()` function calculates the correlation coefficient, which ranges from -1 to 1. A value close to 1 indicates a strong positive relationship, meaning as one variable increases, so does the other. Conversely, a value close to -1 signifies a strong negative relationship, indicating that as one variable increases, the other decreases. A correlation coefficient around 0 suggests no linear relationship between the variables.

```r
correlation_coefficient <- cor(dataset$variable1,
dataset$variable2)
print(correlation_coefficient)
```

Probability distributions are another cornerstone of statistical analysis, providing insights into the likelihood of different outcomes. R supports various probability distributions, including normal (`norm`), binomial (`binom`), and Poisson (`pois`). The `dnorm()`, `dbinom()`, and `dpois()` functions can be used to calculate the densities of these distributions, respectively. Understanding these distributions and their applications is crucial for hypothesis testing and data analysis.

```r
normal_density <- dnorm(x, mean = mean_value, sd = sd_value)
binomial_probability <- dbinom(x, size = trials, prob =
success_probability)
poisson_probability <- dpois(x, lambda = rate)
```

Confidence intervals provide a range of values within which we can expect the true population parameter to lie, with a certain level of confidence. In R, confidence intervals can be calculated for various estimates, including means and proportions. The `t.test()` function, for example, returns a confidence interval for the mean of a sample.

```r
t_test_result <- t.test(dataset$variable)
print(t_test_result$conf.int)
```

Regression analysis is a powerful tool for modeling the relationship between a dependent variable and one or more independent variables. The `lm()` function in R is used for linear regression analysis. It not only estimates the regression coefficients but also provides a comprehensive summary of the regression model, including the R-squared value, which indicates the proportion of variance in the dependent variable that can be explained by the independent variables.

```r
linear_model <- lm(dependent_variable ~ independent_variable1 +
independent_variable2, data = dataset)
summary(linear_model)
```

ANOVA (Analysis of Variance) is used to compare the means of three or more samples. The `aov()` function in R performs ANOVA tests, helping to determine if there are any statistically significant differences between the means of the groups.

```r
anova_result <- aov(dependent_variable ~ group, data = dataset)
summary(anova_result)
```

Non-parametric tests offer an alternative to traditional parametric tests, especially useful when the data do not meet the assumptions required for parametric testing. The `wilcox.test()` function for the Wilcoxon rank-sum test and the `kruskal.test()` function for the Kruskal-Wallis test are examples of non-parametric tests available in R.

```r
wilcox_result <- wilcox.test(variable1, variable2, paired = TRUE)
kruskal_result <- kruskal.test(dependent_variable ~ group, data =
dataset)
```

By leveraging these statistical concepts and tools in R, you can perform a comprehensive analysis of your data, uncovering insights and making informed decisions based on your findings. Whether you're exploring correlations, analyzing probability distributions, estimating confidence intervals, conducting regression analysis, comparing group means, or applying non-parametric tests, R provides a robust framework for statistical analysis, catering to both basic and advanced analytical needs.

Hypothesis Testing

Hypothesis testing in R is a critical step in statistical analysis, allowing researchers to make inferences about populations based on sample data. This process involves several key steps and functions in R that facilitate the testing of hypotheses. The primary goal is to determine whether there is enough evidence in a sample of data to infer that a certain condition holds true for the entire population.

Formulating Hypotheses

The first step in hypothesis testing is to formulate the null hypothesis (H0) and the alternative hypothesis (H1 or Ha). The null hypothesis typically represents a statement of no effect or no difference, while the alternative hypothesis represents a statement of effect, difference, or relationship.

Selecting the Appropriate Test

Depending on the data and the hypotheses, you select an appropriate statistical test. For comparing means, you might use a t-test or ANOVA. For categorical data, a chi-squared test might be appropriate. The choice of test depends on the data type, distribution, and whether the samples are independent or paired.

Performing the Test in R

R provides functions for conducting various statistical tests. For example, to perform a t-test to compare the means of two independent samples, you can use the t.test() function:

```r
t_test_result <- t.test(sample1, sample2)
```

For a chi-squared test to examine the relationship between two categorical variables, you can use:

```r
chi_squared_test_result <- chisq.test(table(variable1, variable2))
```

Interpreting the Results

The output of a hypothesis test in R typically includes a test statistic, a p-value, and sometimes confidence intervals. The p-value represents the probability of observing the test results under the null hypothesis. A small p-value (typically ≤ 0.05) indicates strong evidence against the null hypothesis, leading to its rejection in favor of the alternative hypothesis.

Making Decisions

Based on the p-value, you make a decision regarding the hypotheses. If the p-value is less than or equal to the significance level (α), you reject the null hypothesis. If the p-value is greater than α, you fail to reject the null hypothesis. It's crucial to remember that failing to reject the null hypothesis does not prove it true; it merely indicates insufficient evidence to support the alternative hypothesis.

Assumptions Checking

Many statistical tests assume certain conditions about the data, such as normality or equal variances. Before performing a test, it's important to check these assumptions. For example, the Shapiro-Wilk test can be used to assess normality:

r

```
shapiro_test_result <- shapiro.test(sample_data)
```

And Levene's test can be used to assess the equality of variances:

r

```
levene_test_result <- car::leveneTest(dependent_variable ~
independent_variable, data = dataset)
```

Reporting Results

When reporting the results of a hypothesis test, include the test statistic, the p-value, and the conclusions drawn from the test. It's also important to discuss the implications of these results in the context of the research question or problem being investigated.

Hypothesis testing in R is a powerful tool for statistical analysis, enabling researchers to draw conclusions about populations based on sample data. By carefully selecting the appropriate test, checking assumptions, and correctly interpreting the results, you can make informed decisions and contribute valuable insights to your field of study.

T-tests and ANOVA

T-tests and ANOVA are fundamental tools in hypothesis testing, allowing us to compare means across groups to determine if the observed differences are statistically significant. These tests are pivotal in R for analyzing and interpreting data, providing insights that guide decision-making processes. Let's delve deeper into how to perform these tests in R, ensuring we understand their application and interpretation.

The `t.test()` function in R is versatile, catering to one-sample, paired, and independent two-sample t-tests. For a one-sample t-test, where we compare the mean of a single group against a known mean, the syntax is straightforward:

r

```
one_sample_t_result <- t.test(x = your_data$variable, mu =
known_mean)
```

In this code snippet, `your_data$variable` represents the sample data, and `known_mean` is the mean value you're testing against. The output includes the t-statistic and the p-value, which you'll use to assess the significance of your results.

For comparing the means of two related groups, such as measurements taken before and after a treatment on the same subjects, a paired t-test is appropriate:

r

```
paired_t_result <- t.test(x = pre_treatment_scores, y =
post_treatment_scores, paired = TRUE)
```

Here, `pre_treatment_scores` and `post_treatment_scores` are vectors containing the scores before and after the treatment, respectively. Setting `paired = TRUE` indicates that the data are paired.

When comparing the means of two independent groups, the syntax changes slightly:

r

```
independent_t_result <- t.test(x = group1_data, y = group2_data)
```

`group1_data` and `group2_data` are vectors of the two groups' data. This test assumes equal variances by default, but if you suspect unequal variances (which is common in real-world data), you can add the argument `var.equal = FALSE`.

Moving on to ANOVA, which stands for Analysis of Variance, this test is used when comparing the means of three or more groups. The `aov()` function in R facilitates this analysis:

```r
anova_result <- aov(dependent_variable ~ independent_variable, data
= your_dataframe)
summary(anova_result)
```

In this example, `dependent_variable` is the outcome measure, and `independent_variable` is the factor with three or more levels (groups) you're comparing. The `summary()` function provides the ANOVA table, including the F-statistic and the p-value. A significant p-value indicates that at least one group mean is different from the others. However, ANOVA doesn't tell you which groups are different. To pinpoint the differences, you'll need to conduct post-hoc tests, such as Tukey's HSD (Honestly Significant Difference) test:

```r
tukey_result <- TukeyHSD(anova_result)
```

This code performs Tukey's HSD test on the results of the ANOVA, helping to identify which specific group means differ from each other.

Both t-tests and ANOVA are powerful statistical tools, but their validity hinges on certain assumptions. For t-tests, assumptions include independence of observations, normality of the data distribution, and homogeneity of variances (for independent two-sample t-tests). ANOVA also assumes independence of observations, normality, and equal variances across groups. Before conducting these tests, it's prudent to check these assumptions. For normality, the Shapiro-Wilk test can be used:

```r
shapiro_test_result <- shapiro.test(your_data$variable)
```

And for equal variances, Levene's test is useful:

```r
levene_test_result <- car::leveneTest(dependent_variable ~
independent_variable, data = your_dataframe)
```

These preliminary tests guide the appropriate application of t-tests and ANOVA, ensuring the reliability of your findings. By understanding and applying these statistical tests in R, you can uncover meaningful patterns and differences in your data, providing a solid foundation for further analysis and interpretation.

Chi-squared Tests

The Chi-squared test, denoted as χ^2 test, is a statistical method used to determine if there is a significant difference between the expected frequencies and the observed frequencies in one or more categories. In the realm of R, the `chisq.test()` function is the cornerstone for performing this analysis, allowing us to test hypotheses about the distribution of categorical variables within a population. This test is particularly useful in scenarios such as assessing the effectiveness of a marketing campaign across different demographics or evaluating voting behavior in different regions.

When applying the Chi-squared test, it's crucial to understand its assumptions. Firstly, the data must be categorical. Secondly, the samples or observations should be independent of each other. Lastly, the expected frequency in each category should be at least 5 to ensure the validity of the test results. Violating these assumptions could lead to misleading conclusions.

To perform a Chi-squared test in R, you would typically start by creating a contingency table that summarizes the data. This can be done using the `table()` function, which cross-tabulates the data into a format suitable for the Chi-squared test. For example, if you're analyzing the relationship between two categorical variables, `variable1` and `variable2`, from a dataframe `your_dataframe`, you would create a table as follows:

```r
observed_frequencies <- table(your_dataframe$variable1,
your_dataframe$variable2)
```

Once you have the contingency table, you can perform the Chi-squared test using the `chisq.test()` function:

```r
chi_squared_test_result <- chisq.test(observed_frequencies)
```

This function returns an object containing several pieces of crucial information, including the Chi-squared statistic value, the degrees of freedom associated with the test, and the p-value. The p-value is particularly important as it helps you determine whether the observed differences between the frequencies are statistically significant. A low p-value (typically less than 0.05) indicates that the differences are significant, leading you to reject the null hypothesis, which states that there is no association between the categorical variables.

It's also possible to adjust the `chisq.test()` function for situations where the assumptions of the Chi-squared test might not be fully met. For instance, if the expected frequencies in some of the cells of your contingency table are less than 5, you can apply Yates' continuity correction by setting the `correct` parameter to TRUE:

```r
chi_squared_test_result <- chisq.test(observed_frequencies, correct = TRUE)
```

This correction is particularly recommended for 2x2 tables and can help prevent overestimation of statistical significance.

In addition to testing for independence between two categorical variables, the Chi-squared test can be used for goodness-of-fit tests. This variant of the Chi-squared test compares the observed frequencies of categories against expected frequencies derived from a theoretical distribution. The syntax for a goodness-of-fit test slightly differs, as you need to specify both the observed frequencies and the expected frequencies:

```r
chi_squared_goodness_of_fit_result <- chisq.test(x = observed_frequencies, p = expected_probabilities)
```

Here, `observed_frequencies` is a vector of observed counts, and `expected_probabilities` is a vector of probabilities for each category under the null hypothesis. The degrees of freedom for a goodness-of-fit test are calculated as the number of categories minus one, adjusted for any parameters estimated from the data.

In summary, the Chi-squared test is a versatile tool in R for analyzing categorical data, enabling researchers and data analysts to uncover relationships between variables or assess how well observed data fit with expected distributions. By carefully preparing data, choosing the appropriate form of the Chi-squared test, and interpreting the results in the context of the research question, you can gain valuable insights into the patterns and associations present in your data.

Linear Regression Analysis

Building on our foundation of statistical analysis in R, we delve deeper into **Linear Regression Analysis**, a cornerstone technique for understanding relationships between variables. This method allows us to predict an outcome based on one or more predictors, making it invaluable in many fields, from economics to biology.

To perform a linear regression analysis in R, we use the `lm()` function, which stands for linear model. The basic syntax of `lm()` is straightforward: you specify the formula of the relationship between the dependent variable and one or more independent variables, followed by the dataset containing these variables. The formula typically looks like $y \sim x$, where y is the dependent variable and x is the independent variable.

```R
model <- lm(y ~ x, data = my_data)
```

After fitting the model, it's crucial to review the summary of the model to understand its components, including the intercept, coefficients, R-squared value, and p-values for the predictors. The summary can be accessed using the `summary()` function:

```R
summary(model)
```

The **intercept** represents the expected mean value of y when all x variables are zero. The **coefficients** indicate the expected change in y for a one-unit change in x, holding all other predictors constant. The **R-squared value** measures the proportion of variance in the dependent variable that is predictable from the independent variables, providing insight into the model's explanatory power.

To ensure the model's validity, it's essential to perform diagnostic checks. Diagnostic plots, generated using the `plot()` function, can help identify issues like non-linearity, heteroscedasticity, and outliers:

```R
plot(model)
```

These plots include:

- **Residuals vs Fitted**: Helps check the assumption of linearity and homoscedasticity.

- **Normal Q-Q**: Assesses if the residuals are normally distributed.

- **Scale-Location**: Another check for homoscedasticity.

- **Residuals vs Leverage**: Helps identify influential outliers.

If the assumptions of linear regression are violated, transformations of variables or more complex models may be necessary.

For models with multiple predictors, the syntax of `lm()` expands to include additional independent variables:

```R
multi_model <- lm(y ~ x1 + x2, data = my_data)
```

This model predicts y based on the linear combination of x1 and x2. Interaction terms can also be included to explore how the relationship between one predictor and the outcome changes across levels of another predictor:

```R
interaction_model <- lm(y ~ x1 * x2, data = my_data)
```

In this formula, x1 * x2 includes both the main effects of x1 and x2, and their interaction effect.

Linear regression analysis in R is a powerful tool for data analysis, allowing for both simple and complex models to uncover relationships between variables. By understanding and applying this technique, you can gain deeper insights into your data and make more informed decisions based on predictive modeling.

Model Building and Diagnostics

After fitting a linear model using the `lm()` function in R, it's crucial to assess the model's performance and diagnose any potential issues that could affect its predictive accuracy or interpretability. Model diagnostics play a vital role in this process, helping to ensure that the assumptions underlying linear regression are met. This section delves into the key diagnostic techniques and how to implement them in R, providing a comprehensive guide to refining your linear regression models.

One of the primary assumptions of linear regression is that the residuals, or differences between observed and predicted values, are normally distributed. This can be checked using a Q-Q (quantile-quantile) plot, which compares the distribution of residuals to a normal distribution. In R, this can be accomplished with the `qqnorm()` function applied to the residuals of your model, followed by `qqline()` to add a reference line:

R
```
qqnorm(resid(model))
qqline(resid(model))
```

If the residuals follow the line closely, it suggests that they are normally distributed. Deviations from this line indicate departures from normality, which might necessitate transformations of the dependent variable or the use of alternative models.

Another critical assumption is homoscedasticity, meaning that the variance of the residuals is constant across all levels of the independent variables. This can be visually assessed with a plot of residuals versus fitted values:

R
```
plot(fitted(model), resid(model))
abline(h = 0, lty = 2)
```

In this plot, you're looking for a random scatter of points. Patterns or a funnel shape where the spread of residuals increases or decreases with the fitted values indicate heteroscedasticity. Addressing this might involve transforming the dependent variable or using weighted least squares.

Leverage and Cook's distance are measures used to identify influential observations that have a disproportionate impact on the model. High-leverage points are observations with extreme predictor values, while observations with high Cook's distance can unduly influence the regression coefficients. Both can be identified using diagnostic plots:

R

```
plot(model, which = 4)  # Leverage plot
plot(model, which = 5)  # Cook's distance
```

Observations that stand out in these plots may warrant closer examination. They could be errors, or they might represent valuable data points that are simply unusual. Depending on the context, you might choose to investigate further, exclude them from the analysis, or include additional variables in the model to account for their influence.

Finally, multicollinearity, the occurrence of high correlations among independent variables, can inflate the variance of regression coefficients and make them unstable. The Variance Inflation Factor (VIF) is a common measure to detect multicollinearity. In R, the `vif()` function from the `car` package can be used to calculate VIF values for each predictor in the model:

R

```
library(car)
vif(model)
```

VIF values greater than 5 (or 10, according to some sources) suggest that multicollinearity may be a concern, indicating that the model might benefit from the removal or consolidation of some variables.

By carefully examining these diagnostic measures and plots, you can identify and address issues in your linear regression model, improving its accuracy and reliability. Remember, the goal of diagnostics is not just to validate the model but to understand it better and ensure that it accurately represents the underlying data and relationships.

Predictions and Residuals

After understanding the basics of model diagnostics, the next step in linear regression analysis is to utilize the model for **predictions** and to analyze the **residuals**. These two components are crucial for interpreting the model's effectiveness and for making informed decisions based on the model's outputs.

Making Predictions

Predictions in R using a linear model can be performed with the `predict()` function. This function requires the model object and, optionally, a new dataset for which predictions are desired. If no new data is provided, predictions are made for the dataset used to fit the model. Here's how to use it:

R

```
# Assuming 'model' is your linear model object
predictions <- predict(model, newdata = new_dataset)
```

This line of code generates predictions based on `new_dataset`, which should have the same predictors used to train the model. The output, `predictions`, contains the predicted values of the dependent variable.

Analyzing Residuals

Residuals, the differences between observed and predicted values, are key to understanding the model's accuracy. Analyzing residuals helps in identifying patterns that might indicate issues with the model, such as non-linearity or outliers. In R, residuals can be extracted using the `resid()` function:

R

```
residuals <- resid(model)
```

A common practice is to plot these residuals against the fitted (predicted) values to visually inspect any systematic patterns. A well-fitted model should display a random scatter of residuals, indicating homoscedasticity.

R

```
plot(fitted(model), residuals)
abline(h = 0, col = "red")
```

In this plot, the horizontal line at zero helps in identifying deviations from randomness. Patterns or trends in this plot suggest that the model may not be capturing some aspect of the data's structure, possibly requiring model refinement or the inclusion of additional variables.

Residual Standard Error

Another important metric to consider is the **Residual Standard Error** (RSE), which measures the average amount that the response will deviate from the true regression line. It is calculated as the square root of the reduced sum of squares of residuals. While RSE is not directly provided in the summary output of `lm()`, it can be computed as follows:

R

```
rse <- sqrt(sum(resid(model)^2) / model$df.residual)
```

RSE provides a measure of the model's lack of fit to the data in the units of the response variable, offering a quantitative assessment of prediction accuracy.

Leveraging Predictions and Residuals

Predictions and residuals are not just end products of regression analysis but are tools for iterative model improvement. By analyzing residuals for patterns and calculating prediction accuracy metrics like RSE, you can identify areas where the model may be lacking. This iterative process of model evaluation, diagnostics, and refinement is key to developing robust predictive models in R.

Remember, the goal of regression analysis is not just to fit a model to the data but to develop a model that can accurately predict new, unseen data. Through careful examination of predictions and residuals, you can ensure that your model is both accurate and reliable, making it a powerful tool for data analysis and decision-making.

Introduction to Machine Learning in R

Machine learning in R provides a comprehensive suite of tools and methods for analyzing complex datasets and making predictions or decisions without being explicitly programmed to perform the task. R, being a statistical programming language, is naturally suited for these tasks, offering libraries such as `caret`, `nnet`, `randomForest`, and `e1071` for implementing machine learning algorithms. The process of applying machine learning in R involves several key steps: data preprocessing, feature selection, model choice, model training, evaluation, and tuning.

Data Preprocessing is crucial in machine learning to improve the quality of data and the efficiency of analysis. This step includes handling missing values, normalizing or scaling features, and encoding categorical variables. For instance, to scale a dataset in R, you can use the `scale()` function, which standardizes the data to have a mean of zero and a standard deviation of one.

R

```
scaled_data <- scale(original_data)
```

Feature Selection involves identifying the most relevant features to use in model training. This step is essential because irrelevant or redundant features can decrease the model's performance. The `caret` package provides functions like `rfe()` (Recursive Feature Elimination) to automate this process.

R

```
library(caret)
control <- rfeControl(functions=rfFuncs, method="cv", number=10)
results <- rfe(training_features, training_labels, sizes=c(1:5),
rfeControl=control)
```

Model Choice is about selecting the appropriate algorithm for your specific problem. R offers a wide range of machine learning models, from linear regression for continuous outcomes to logistic regression for binary outcomes, and more complex algorithms like support vector machines (SVM), decision trees, and random forests for classification and regression tasks.

Model Training is the process of feeding the selected model with data so that it can learn the patterns. This is typically done using the `train()` function from the `caret` package, which also allows for easy cross-validation and hyperparameter tuning.

R

```
model <- train(training_features, training_labels, method = "rf",
trControl = trainControl(method = "cv"))
```

Evaluation of the model involves assessing its performance on a test set to ensure it generalizes well to new, unseen data. Common metrics for evaluation include accuracy, precision, recall, and the F1 score for classification tasks, and RMSE (Root Mean Squared Error) for regression tasks.

R

```
predictions <- predict(model, newdata=test_features)
confusionMatrix(predictions, test_labels)
```

Tuning the model is the final step, where you adjust the hyperparameters to improve the model's performance. The `caret` package's `train()` function can also perform this task by specifying a grid of possible values for each hyperparameter and evaluating each combination's performance.

R

```
tuneGrid <- expand.grid(.mtry=c(1:5))
tuned_model <- train(training_features, training_labels, method =
"rf", tuneGrid = tuneGrid, trControl = trainControl(method = "cv"))
```

Machine learning in R is a powerful approach for data analysis, offering the flexibility to handle a wide range of data types and complexities. By following these steps and utilizing R's extensive packages and functions, you can develop predictive models that can uncover hidden insights and make accurate predictions from your data.

Supervised vs. Unsupervised Learning

In the realm of machine learning within R, two primary learning paradigms stand out: supervised and unsupervised learning. Each of these paradigms plays a crucial role in how models are constructed, trained, and applied to datasets to extract meaningful patterns or predictions. Understanding the distinctions and applications of these learning types is fundamental for anyone delving into machine learning with R.

Supervised learning is characterized by its use of labeled datasets. These datasets provide the model with both input data and the corresponding output. The goal of supervised learning is to train a model so accurately that when new, unseen data is introduced, the model can predict the output based on the learning from the training dataset. Common supervised learning tasks include classification, where the output is a category, and regression, where the output is a continuous value. In R, supervised learning can be implemented using various packages such as `caret`, `nnet`, and `randomForest`. For instance, to perform a linear regression, which predicts a continuous value based on one or more input features, you can use the `lm()` function:

```R
R
model <- lm(y ~ x1 + x2, data = my_data)
```

This code snippet demonstrates how to train a linear model predicting `y` from `x1` and `x2`. The `lm()` function is a straightforward example of supervised learning, aiming to find the linear relationship between the dependent variable `y` and independent variables `x1` and `x2`.

On the other hand, unsupervised learning involves working with datasets that do not have labeled responses. The model learns through the inherent structure of the data without any explicit instructions on what patterns to find. Unsupervised learning is typically used for clustering, dimensionality reduction, and association tasks. Clustering groups similar data points together, dimensionality reduction simplifies data without losing critical information, and association rules identify items that frequently co-occur. The `kmeans()` function in R, for example, allows for clustering:

```R
R
set.seed(123) # Setting seed for reproducibility
clusters <- kmeans(my_data, centers = 3)
```

This code performs k-means clustering on `my_data`, aiming to find three distinct clusters within the dataset. Unlike supervised learning, where the goal is to predict an outcome, unsupervised learning in this context seeks to uncover hidden patterns or groupings in the data without prior knowledge of what those groupings might be.

Both supervised and unsupervised learning have their unique challenges and applications. Supervised learning models are only as good as the labels provided in the training data. Poorly labeled data can lead to inaccurate models, while high-quality labels can be expensive or time-consuming to obtain. Unsupervised learning, while freeing from the need for labeled data, can sometimes produce results that are difficult to interpret, requiring domain knowledge to make sense of the clusters or patterns identified by the model.

In practice, the choice between supervised and unsupervised learning depends on the nature of the problem at hand, the type of data available, and the specific goals of the analysis. R provides a comprehensive toolkit for both learning paradigms, offering functions and packages that cater to a wide array of machine learning tasks. Whether predicting future trends with supervised learning or uncovering hidden structures in data with unsupervised learning, R equips users with the necessary tools to tackle complex data analysis challenges.

Building a Simple Model

Building a simple model in R involves a series of steps that guide you from preparing your data to evaluating the model's performance. After ensuring your dataset is clean and preprocessed, the next step is to split your data into training and testing sets. This is crucial for assessing how well your model generalizes to new, unseen data. The `caret` package in R simplifies this process with functions designed for creating predictive models.

R

```
library(caret)
set.seed(123) # Ensure reproducibility
index <- createDataPartition(y, p = .8, list = FALSE)
trainData <- my_data[index, ]
testData <- my_data[-index, ]
```

In this snippet, `createDataPartition(y, p = .8, list = FALSE)` randomly partitions the dataset, with 80% of the data allocated for training and the remaining 20% for testing. `y` represents the dependent variable in your dataset, and `my_data` is your full dataset. This split ensures that you have a separate dataset to train and another to test the model's predictions.

Once your data is split, you can proceed to build a simple model. For beginners, starting with a linear regression model is often recommended due to its simplicity and interpretability. The `lm()` function in R makes it straightforward to fit a linear model.

R

```
simpleModel <- lm(y ~ ., data = trainData)
```

This code fits a linear model (`simpleModel`) using all other variables in `trainData` as predictors for `y`, the dependent variable. The `.` symbol indicates that all other variables in the dataset should be used as predictors.

After fitting the model, it's important to evaluate its performance. The `summary()` function provides a comprehensive overview of your model's statistics, including coefficients, significance levels, and the R-squared value, which indicates how well the model explains the variability of the response data.

R

```
summary(simpleModel)
```

However, understanding the model's performance on the training data is not enough. You must assess how well it predicts new, unseen data. This is where your test dataset comes into play. Use the `predict()` function to make predictions on the test set and compare these predictions to the actual values.

R

```
predictions <- predict(simpleModel, newdata = testData)
```

To quantify the model's accuracy, calculate metrics such as Mean Absolute Error (MAE) or Root Mean Squared Error (RMSE). These metrics provide insight into the average error in the predictions.

R

```
MAE <- mean(abs(predictions - testData$y))
RMSE <- sqrt(mean((predictions - testData$y)^2))
```

These calculations give you a numerical value representing the average error (MAE) and the standard deviation of the errors (RMSE) between your model's predictions and the actual values. Lower values indicate a better fit to the data.

Remember, building a model is an iterative process. Based on the performance metrics, you may need to return to earlier steps, perhaps selecting different variables, transforming variables, or even trying different types of models. The `caret` package also offers functions for more advanced modeling techniques and automated tuning of model parameters, which can further improve your model's performance.

By following these steps and utilizing R's comprehensive suite of tools, you can build, evaluate, and refine simple models, laying the foundation for more complex analyses and predictive modeling projects.

CHAPTER 6

R Programming Essentials

In this section, we delve into the intricacies of **writing functions in R**, a fundamental skill that enhances the power and flexibility of your data analysis. Functions in R allow you to encapsulate a sequence of commands into a single command, making your code more modular, reusable, and easier to read. The basic structure of a function in R is straightforward, yet it opens the door to advanced data manipulation and analysis techniques.

To define a function in R, you use the `function()` keyword. The syntax is as follows:

```R
my_function <- function(arg1, arg2, ...) {
  # Code to execute
  return(result)
}
```

Here, `my_function` is the name of your function, `arg1`, `arg2`, ... are the arguments passed to the function, and `result` is the output of the function. The `return()` function is used to specify the output of your function explicitly, although R will automatically return the result of the last line of code executed in the function if `return()` is not used.

Let's consider a simple example to illustrate the concept. Suppose you want to create a function that calculates the square of a number. Your function might look like this:

```R
square <- function(x) {
```

```
    return(x^2)
}
```

You can then use this function just like any other function in R:

```
R

square(4)
# [1] 16
```

This example is simple, yet it demonstrates the power of functions in R. By encapsulating the operation within a function, you've made your code more readable and reusable. You can now easily square any number without having to rewrite the squaring operation each time.

Beyond simple operations, functions in R can perform complex data manipulations involving multiple steps and conditional logic. For instance, you might write a function that takes a data frame and a column name as arguments, checks for missing values in that column, and returns a summary of the missing data. This is just a glimpse of what's possible when you start to leverage the power of functions in R.

As you become more comfortable with writing functions, you'll find that they are an indispensable tool in your R programming arsenal. They not only make your code more organized and readable but also enable you to tackle more complex data analysis tasks with ease.

When diving deeper into the realm of functions in R, it's crucial to understand the concept of **scope**. Scope refers to the part of your R script where a variable is accessible. Variables defined inside a function are local to that function and are not accessible outside of it. This encapsulation is beneficial for avoiding conflicts with variables in other parts of your script. For example:

```
R

add_numbers <- function(a, b) {
  result <- a + b
  return(result)
}
# result is not accessible here and will throw an error if called
```

Another powerful feature of R functions is the ability to set **default values** for arguments. This makes your functions more flexible and easier to use. If an argument is not provided by the user, the function will use the default value. Here's how you can define a function with default values:

R

```
multiply_numbers <- function(a, b = 2) {
   return(a * b)
}
# This will use the default value of b
multiply_numbers(4)
# [1] 8
```

Vectorization is a concept that R excels at and can significantly enhance the performance of your functions. Many functions in R are vectorized, meaning they can operate on an entire vector of values at once. When writing your functions, leveraging vectorized operations can lead to more efficient and concise code. For instance, the `square` function we defined earlier is naturally vectorized because the ^ operator in R is vectorized:

R

```
square(c(2, 4, 6))
# [1] 4 16 36
```

Error handling is another critical aspect of writing robust R functions. R provides several mechanisms for dealing with errors and exceptional conditions in your code. The `stop()` function can be used to generate an error if a condition is not met, while `warning()` can be used to provide a less severe alert to the user without stopping the execution of the function. Here's an example of using `stop()` to enforce that an input must be numeric:

R

```
safe_divide <- function(a, b) {
   if(!is.numeric(a) || !is.numeric(b)) {
      stop("Both arguments must be numeric")
   }
   return(a / b)
```

```
}
```

Lastly, **debugging** functions in R can sometimes be challenging, especially as your functions grow in complexity. Utilizing the `browser()` function within your function can pause execution at a specific point, allowing you to inspect variables and step through the code line by line. This can be invaluable for identifying and fixing issues in your functions.

R

```
troubleshoot_function <- function(x) {
  if(x > 10) {
    browser() # Execution will pause here if x > 10
  }
  return(x^2)
}
```

By mastering these advanced aspects of function writing in R—scope, default values, vectorization, error handling, and debugging—you'll be well-equipped to tackle a wide range of programming challenges. Functions are the building blocks of R programming, and with these skills, you can start building more efficient, robust, and reusable R code.

Writing Functions in R

Functions in R are not just about performing calculations or manipulating data; they also offer a way to implement **control structures** within them, allowing for more dynamic and flexible code execution. Control structures such as `if-else` statements and `for` loops can be embedded within functions to perform different actions based on certain conditions or to iterate over a set of values, respectively. This capability significantly enhances the functionality and applicability of custom functions in various data analysis scenarios.

Consider a scenario where you need to process a dataset with conditional logic. You might want to apply a specific transformation to a column based on the values in another column. Here's how you could write a function incorporating an `if-else` statement to achieve this:

R

```
transform_data <- function(data, column1, column2) {
```

```
  for (i in 1:nrow(data)) {
    if (data[i, column1] > 0) {
       data[i, column2] <- log(data[i, column2])
    } else {
       data[i, column2] <- sqrt(data[i, column2])
    }
  }
  return(data)
}
```

In this example, the function `transform_data` takes a dataframe `data` and the names of two columns as arguments. It iterates over each row of the dataframe, applying a logarithmic transformation to the second column if the value in the first column is positive, and a square root transformation otherwise. This function showcases how control structures can be used within functions to apply complex, conditional data transformations.

Another powerful aspect of writing functions in R is the use of **loops**. Loops can be particularly useful when you need to perform repetitive tasks or operations on a series of elements. Here's an example of a function that uses a `for` loop to calculate the factorial of a number:

R

```
factorial <- function(n) {
  result <- 1
  for (i in 1:n) {
    result <- result * i
  }
  return(result)
}
```

This `factorial` function calculates the product of all positive integers up to `n`, demonstrating how loops can be incorporated into functions for iterative calculations.

When writing functions that include control structures, it's essential to ensure that your code is well-organized and clear. Comments can be added to explain the purpose of certain blocks of code or the logic behind a particular control structure. This practice not only makes your code more readable but also easier to debug and maintain.

In addition to `if-else` statements and `for` loops, R also supports other control structures such as `while` loops and `switch` statements, which can be used within functions to further enhance their flexibility and power. By mastering these concepts, you can write more sophisticated and efficient R functions that can handle a wide range of data processing and analysis tasks.

Remember, the key to effective function writing in R is not just about the syntax but understanding how to structure your code to make it as efficient, readable, and reusable as possible. Incorporating control structures into your functions is a significant step towards achieving this goal, enabling you to tackle more complex data analysis challenges with confidence.

Control Structures

In the realm of R programming, **control structures** play a pivotal role in managing the flow of execution. These structures allow for conditional execution of code segments, iteration over collections, and branching of execution paths based on logical conditions. Understanding and effectively utilizing these constructs can significantly enhance the functionality and efficiency of your R scripts.

If-Else Statements

The `if-else` statement is a fundamental control structure that executes a block of code if a specified condition is true and optionally executes another block if the condition is false. The basic syntax is as follows:

R
```
if (condition) {
  # code to execute if condition is true
} else {
  # code to execute if condition is false
}
```

For example, to check if a number is positive and print a message accordingly, you could write:

```R
number <- -5
if (number > 0) {
  print("The number is positive.")
} else {
  print("The number is not positive.")
}
```

Else If Ladder

For scenarios requiring multiple conditions to be checked, an else if ladder can be used. This allows for sequential evaluation of conditions:

```R
if (condition1) {
  # code if condition1 is true
} else if (condition2) {
  # code if condition2 is true
} else {
  # code if none of the above conditions are true
}
```

For Loops

The for loop is used to iterate over a sequence, such as vectors or lists, and execute a block of code for each element in the sequence. The syntax is:

```R
for (variable in sequence) {
  # code to execute
}
```

For instance, to print each element of a vector:

```R
vec <- c(1, 2, 3, 4, 5)
for (val in vec) {
  print(val)
}
```

While Loops

A `while` loop continues to execute a block of code as long as a specified condition remains true. Its syntax is:

```R
while (condition) {
  # code to execute
}
```

For example, to count down from 5 to 1:

```R
count <- 5
while (count > 0) {
  print(count)
  count <- count - 1
}
```

Repeat Loops

The `repeat` loop executes a block of code indefinitely until a break condition is explicitly called. This is useful for loops where the termination condition is not known in advance:

```R
x <- 1
repeat {
  print(x)
  x <- x + 1
```

```r
  if (x > 5) {
    break
  }
}
```

Break and Next

Within loop constructs, `break` is used to exit the loop prematurely, while `next` skips the rest of the current iteration and proceeds to the next iteration:

```r
R
for (i in 1:10) {
  if (i == 5) {
    next
  }
  if (i == 8) {
    break
  }
  print(i)
}
```

In this example, the number 5 is skipped due to the `next` statement, and the loop terminates when i equals 8 because of the `break` statement.

Switch Statements

The `switch` statement is a control structure used to execute different blocks of code based on the value of a single expression. It is particularly useful for simplifying complex if-else chains:

```r
R
x <- "two"
result <- switch(x,
                 "one" = 1,
                 "two" = 2,
                 "three" = 3,
```

```
                         0)
print(result)
```

This prints 2 as x matches the second case.

By mastering these control structures, you can write more dynamic, efficient, and readable R code. Each structure serves a unique purpose, enabling you to handle various programming scenarios with ease. Whether it's conditional execution with `if-else`, iterating with `for` or `while` loops, or managing execution flow with `break` and `next`, these constructs are indispensable tools in your R programming toolkit.

If-Else Statements

The `if-else` statement in R is a powerful tool for making decisions within your code based on conditions. It allows you to execute different blocks of code depending on whether a condition is true or false. This control structure is fundamental in programming, enabling you to add logic to your R scripts that can handle a wide variety of situations, from simple value checks to complex decision-making processes involving data.

To use an `if-else` statement, you need to understand its basic syntax. The condition within the `if` statement is evaluated, and if the condition is TRUE, the code block immediately following the condition is executed. If the condition is FALSE, the code block after the `else` keyword is executed. Here's a simple example:

```r
x <- 20
if (x > 10) {
  print("x is greater than 10")
} else {
  print("x is not greater than 10")
}
```

In this example, the output will be "x is greater than 10" because the condition x > 10 evaluates to TRUE. The `if-else` statement directly controls which block of code is executed based on the condition's truth value.

For situations where you need to evaluate multiple conditions, R provides the `else if` statement, allowing you to chain multiple conditions together. This is particularly useful when you have more than two possible outcomes based on the conditions you're checking. Here's how you might use `else if` to add another condition to the previous example:

```r
x <- 20
if (x > 20) {
  print("x is greater than 20")
} else if (x > 10) {
  print("x is greater than 10 but not greater than 20")
} else {
  print("x is not greater than 10")
}
```

In this case, the output will be "x is greater than 10 but not greater than 20" because the first condition x > 20 is FALSE, but the second condition x > 10 is TRUE. The `else` part would only execute if all preceding conditions were FALSE.

It's important to note that R evaluates the conditions in an `if-else if-else` chain sequentially and will execute the code block for the first TRUE condition it encounters. After executing the corresponding code block, it will exit the control structure and not evaluate any further conditions.

When working with `if-else` statements, especially with complex conditions, readability can become an issue. To maintain readability, you should:

- Use proper indentation to make the structure of your `if-else` statements clear.

- Keep conditions as simple and readable as possible, possibly by defining complex conditions beforehand and storing them in variables.

- Comment your code, especially for the logic behind each condition, so that others (and you in the future) can understand the decision-making process in your script.

Here's an example of using variables to simplify conditions:

```r
r
is_adult <- age >= 18
has_permission <- TRUE
if (is_adult && has_permission) {
  print("Access granted")
} else {
  print("Access denied")
}
```

In this example, the logical condition combines two variables with the logical AND operator (`&&`). This makes the `if` statement easier to read and understand at a glance.

`if-else` statements are a cornerstone of programming in R, enabling you to write flexible and dynamic code. Whether you're filtering data, setting values based on conditions, or implementing complex decision trees, mastering `if-else` statements will significantly enhance your ability to analyze data and implement algorithms in R.

Loops

Loops in R are powerful constructs that enable you to automate repetitive tasks, making your code more efficient and your data analysis process more streamlined. Understanding how to effectively use loops can significantly enhance your ability to handle complex data manipulation and analysis tasks. In R, there are primarily two types of loops that you will find yourself using frequently: `for` loops and `while` loops.

`for` Loops

A `for` loop is used to iterate over a sequence, such as a vector, list, or even a data frame, and execute a block of code for each element in the sequence. The basic syntax of a `for` loop in R is as follows:

```r
R
for (variable in sequence) {
  # code to execute
}
```

Here's an example of using a `for` loop to iterate over a vector and print each element:

```R
numbers <- c(1, 2, 3, 4, 5)
for (number in numbers) {
  print(number)
}
```

This loop will print each number in the `numbers` vector to the console. `for` loops are incredibly versatile and can be used for a wide range of tasks, including modifying data frames, performing calculations on lists of numbers, and more.

`while` Loops

A `while` loop continues to execute as long as a specified condition is TRUE. The syntax for a `while` loop is:

```R
while (condition) {
  # code to execute
}
```

An example of a `while` loop in action is:

```R
count <- 1
while (count <= 5) {
  print(count)
  count <- count + 1
}
```

This loop will print the numbers 1 through 5 to the console. `while` loops are particularly useful when you do not know in advance how many times you need to execute a block of code. However, it's crucial to ensure that the loop has a condition that will eventually become FALSE; otherwise, you may create an infinite loop that will continue to run indefinitely.

Loop Control Statements

R also provides loop control statements that give you more control over the execution of your loops. These include `break` and `next`.

- `break` is used to exit a loop prematurely. It is typically used within a conditional statement to exit the loop if a certain condition is met.

R
```
for (i in 1:10) {
  if (i == 6) {
    break
  }
  print(i)
}
```

This loop will print the numbers 1 through 5 and then exit the loop when `i` equals 6.

- `next` is used to skip the rest of the current iteration and proceed to the next iteration of the loop.

R
```
for (i in 1:5) {
  if (i == 3) {
    next
  }
  print(i)
}
```

In this example, the number 3 will be skipped, and the loop will print 1, 2, 4, and 5.

Applying Loops to Data Frames

Loops can be particularly useful when working with data frames in R. For instance, you might want to apply a function to each column of a data frame or filter rows based on certain criteria. Here's an example of using a `for` loop to calculate the mean of each column in a data frame:

```R
data <- data.frame(a = 1:4, b = 2:5, c = 3:6)
means <- numeric(ncol(data))
for (i in 1:ncol(data)) {
  means[i] <- mean(data[[i]])
}
print(means)
```

This loop calculates the mean of each column in the data data frame and stores the results in the means vector.

Loops are a fundamental aspect of programming in R that can greatly simplify and automate the process of data manipulation and analysis. By mastering for and while loops, along with loop control statements like break and next, you can write more efficient and effective R code.

Error Handling and Debugging

Error handling and debugging are critical components of programming in R that ensure your code runs smoothly and is free from bugs. When writing functions or scripts, it's inevitable to encounter errors. Understanding how to manage these errors and debug your code effectively can save you time and frustration.

Error Handling in R

R provides several functions to handle errors gracefully. The most common approach is using the tryCatch() function, which allows you to execute code that might fail and define a way to handle errors without stopping the execution of your program. Here's a basic structure:

```R
result <- tryCatch({
  # Code that might produce an error
  error_prone_function()
}, error = function(e) {
  # Code to handle the error
```

```
  cat("An error occurred:", e$message, "\n")
})
```

In this example, if `error_prone_function()` fails, the error handling function prints the error message instead of stopping the script. This approach is particularly useful in data analysis pipelines where you want to log errors without halting execution for every minor issue.

Another useful function for error handling is `try()`, which is a simplified version of `tryCatch()`. It runs a piece of code and returns an error object if the code fails, which you can then inspect or ignore. This is useful for quick checks and when you're experimenting with R code:

R
```
result <- try(log(-1))
if(inherits(result, "try-error")) {
   cat("Failed to compute log: ", result, "\n")
}
```

Debugging in R

Debugging is the process of identifying and fixing errors or bugs in your code. R provides several tools for debugging, which can help you understand where and why your code is not behaving as expected.

1. `browser()`: This function inserts a breakpoint in your function or script. When R executes this line, it pauses, and you can manually inspect variables, step through the code, and evaluate expressions.

R
```
my_function <- function(x) {
  if(x > 10) {
    browser()
  }
  x^2
}
```

2. `traceback()`: After an error occurs, calling `traceback()` shows the sequence of function calls that led to the error. This is helpful to trace the error's origin in complex scripts.

3. `debug()`: This function allows you to step through the execution of another function interactively. R will pause at the beginning of the function, and you can proceed line by line.

R

```
debug(my_function)
my_function(15)
```

4. `print()` and `cat()` statements: Sometimes, simply printing variables at different points in your code can help identify where things go wrong. This is a basic but effective strategy for simple debugging tasks.

5. **RStudio's built-in debugger**: If you're using RStudio, it offers a graphical debugger that integrates with the above tools, making it easier to set breakpoints, inspect variables, and step through your code.

When debugging, start by isolating where the problem might be occurring. Use `traceback()` to find the function call that caused the error, then use `browser()` or `debug()` to step through the suspect function. Pay close attention to the values of variables and the flow of execution to pinpoint the issue.

Remember, error handling and debugging are skills that improve with practice. The more you work with R, the better you'll become at anticipating potential errors and quickly resolving issues when they arise. By leveraging R's error handling functions and debugging tools, you can write more robust and reliable R code, making your data analysis projects smoother and more efficient.

Efficient R Programming

Efficient R programming involves understanding and implementing practices that make your R code run faster and more efficiently. This can significantly reduce the execution time of your scripts, especially when dealing with large datasets or complex computations. Here are some strategies to enhance the efficiency of your R programming:

1. Vectorization: One of the most powerful features of R is its ability to operate on entire vectors of data at once, rather than looping over elements one by one. Whenever possible, use vectorized functions to perform operations on whole datasets. For example, consider the difference between using a `for` loop to calculate the square of each number in a vector versus using the vectorized function `^`:

```r
# Less efficient
squares <- numeric(length = 100)
for (i in 1:100) {
  squares[i] <- i^2
}
# More efficient
squares <- (1:100)^2
```

2. Avoiding Loops: Loops in R, such as `for`, `while`, and `repeat`, can be very slow, especially when they involve large iterations. Try to use R's apply functions (`lapply`, `sapply`, `vapply`, `tapply`) as they are often faster and more concise. These functions can apply a function over elements or slices of data structures efficiently:

```r
# Calculate the mean of each column in a dataframe
column_means <- apply(X = mtcars, MARGIN = 2, FUN = mean)
```

3. Pre-allocating Memory: When you know the size of the object you're creating, pre-allocate the memory for it. Growing an object iteratively (e.g., within a loop) can be very inefficient because R has to find new space for the object with each iteration:

```r
# Pre-allocate a vector
result <- vector("numeric", length = 100)
for (i in 1:100) {
  result[i] <- sqrt(i)
}
```

4. Using Efficient Data Structures: Different data structures can significantly impact the performance of your R code. For example, operations on `data.table` objects are usually much faster than equivalent operations on `data.frame` objects. Consider using more efficient data structures where appropriate:

```r
library(data.table)
DT <- data.table(mtcars)
mean_mpg <- DT[, .(mean_mpg = mean(mpg))]
```

5. Profiling Your R Code: Use R's built-in profiling tools like `Rprof` to identify bottlenecks in your code. Profiling allows you to see where your code spends most of its time, helping you to focus your optimization efforts where they are most needed:

```r
Rprof()
# Run your R code here
Rprof(NULL)
summaryRprof()
```

6. Parallel Processing: For operations that can be performed independently, consider using parallel processing to distribute the work across multiple CPU cores. The `parallel` package in R provides functions for parallel execution that can significantly reduce computation time for suitable tasks:

```r
library(parallel)
no_cores <- detectCores() - 1
result <- mclapply(1:100, function(x) sqrt(x), mc.cores = no_cores)
```

Implementing these strategies can lead to significant improvements in the performance of your R scripts. Remember, the key to efficient R programming is not just writing code that works but writing code that works fast and efficiently, especially as the size of your data grows.

Vectorization

Understanding the concept of vectorization in R extends beyond merely replacing loops with vectorized operations. It's about embracing a mindset that leverages R's strengths to write concise, readable, and efficient code. Let's delve deeper into how vectorization can be applied in more complex scenarios and the benefits it brings to your R programming practices.

Consider a scenario where you're working with a dataset that requires the application of a function across multiple columns. Instead of iterating through each column with a loop, vectorization allows you to apply the function simultaneously across columns, significantly reducing the execution time. For instance, if you want to standardize the values in a dataframe (subtract the mean and divide by the standard deviation), vectorization makes this task straightforward:

```r
standardize <- function(x) {
  (x - mean(x)) / sd(x)
}
df <- data.frame(a = rnorm(100), b = rnorm(100), c = rnorm(100))
df_standardized <- as.data.frame(lapply(df, standardize))
```

In this example, `lapply` is used to apply the `standardize` function across each column of the dataframe `df`. This approach is not only efficient but also clear and concise, showcasing the power of vectorization in R.

Another aspect of vectorization is the use of vectorized functions for conditional operations. The `ifelse` function in R is a vectorized alternative to the `if-else` statement, allowing you to perform element-wise operations based on a condition. For example, replacing negative values in a vector with zero can be efficiently done with `ifelse`:

```r
numbers <- c(-1, 2, -3, 4, -5, 6)
positive_numbers <- ifelse(numbers < 0, 0, numbers)
```

This code snippet demonstrates how `ifelse` processes each element of the `numbers` vector, replacing negative values with zero, in a single, swift operation. This is a clear advantage over writing a loop to iterate through each element and conditionally replace values.

Vectorization also plays a crucial role in mathematical operations involving matrices and arrays. R's ability to perform element-wise operations on these data structures without explicit loops is a testament to the language's efficiency. For instance, multiplying two matrices element-wise can be achieved with the * operator directly:

```r
matrix1 <- matrix(1:9, nrow = 3)
matrix2 <- matrix(9:1, nrow = 3)
product_matrix <- matrix1 * matrix2
```

This operation multiplies corresponding elements of `matrix1` and `matrix2`, showcasing how vectorized operations simplify complex mathematical tasks.

In summary, vectorization is a cornerstone of efficient R programming, enabling you to write faster, cleaner, and more expressive code. By leveraging vectorized operations, you can avoid the overhead of loops, making your R scripts more performant and easier to maintain. Whether you're manipulating data frames, performing conditional operations, or working with matrices, embracing vectorization will transform the way you approach programming in R.

Applying Functions

The power of R programming is significantly amplified when you master the art of applying functions to data structures. This capability allows for more sophisticated data manipulation and analysis, enabling you to execute complex operations with minimal code. A deeper understanding of `apply` family functions, including `lapply`, `sapply`, `vapply`, and `tapply`, is essential for efficient data processing.

`lapply` and `sapply` are particularly useful for lists and vectors. `lapply` returns a list of the same length as the input, applying a function to each element. For example, to calculate the length of each string in a character vector, you can use:

```r
words <- c("apple", "banana", "cherry")
lengths <- lapply(words, nchar)
```

`lengths` will be a list where each element is the length of the corresponding string in `words`. If you prefer a vector result, `sapply` is the more suitable choice:

```r
lengths_vector <- sapply(words, nchar)
```

`vapply` is a variant of `sapply` that allows for a more rigid specification of the return value, enhancing the safety of your code by ensuring the output type is as expected. For instance, to ensure that the output is always an integer vector, you can specify it explicitly:

```r
lengths_vector_strict <- vapply(words, nchar, integer(1))
```

This ensures that the function `nchar` applied to each element of `words` returns an integer vector of length 1, providing a safeguard against unexpected output types.

`apply` is typically used for matrices and arrays, where you specify the margin (1 for rows, 2 for columns) to apply a function across. For example, to calculate the sum of each column in a matrix:

```r
matrix_data <- matrix(1:9, nrow = 3)
column_sums <- apply(matrix_data, 2, sum)
```

This will return a vector containing the sum of each column in `matrix_data`. The flexibility of `apply` makes it a powerful tool for matrix operations.

`mapply` is a multivariate version of `sapply`, allowing you to apply a function to multiple arguments. Suppose you have two vectors and you want to apply a function to the corresponding elements of each vector:

```r
vector1 <- 1:5
```

```r
vector2 <- 6:10
sums <- mapply(sum, vector1, vector2)
```

This will return a vector where each element is the sum of the corresponding elements in `vector1` and `vector2`.

`tapply` is used for applying a function over subsets of a vector, categorized by another vector, often useful in statistical data analysis. For example, to calculate the mean of a numeric vector based on a grouping factor:

```r
set.seed(123)
values <- rnorm(10)
groups <- gl(2, 5, labels = c("Group 1", "Group 2"))
group_means <- tapply(values, groups, mean)
```

This will calculate the mean of `values` for each level in `groups`, returning a vector of means for "Group 1" and "Group 2".

Mastering these functions allows you to write concise, efficient R code that can perform complex data manipulation tasks. By applying functions across vectors, lists, matrices, and data frames, you can streamline your data analysis workflows, making your R programming more effective and your data analysis insights more profound.

CHAPTER 7

Working with Text Data

In the realm of **R programming**, working with text data is a critical skill, especially given the vast amount of unstructured data generated daily. The `stringr` package in R provides a cohesive set of functions designed to make string manipulation both straightforward and intuitive. When dealing with text data, understanding and applying these functions can significantly enhance your data analysis capabilities.

String Manipulation with stringr

The `stringr` package is part of the tidyverse, and it simplifies string operations by ensuring that all functions deal with strings in a consistent manner. To start using `stringr`, you first need to install and load the package:

```r
install.packages("stringr")
library(stringr)
```

One of the most common tasks in text data analysis is extracting specific patterns from strings. The `str_extract()` function allows you to pull out matches to a pattern:

```r
text <- "The quick brown fox jumps over the lazy dog"
pattern <- "quick brown fox"
str_extract(text, pattern)
```

This will return the exact match to the pattern if found in the text. For more complex patterns, regular expressions (regex) can be used to specify the search criteria.

Regular Expressions

Regular expressions are a powerful tool for pattern matching and text manipulation. They can seem daunting at first, but mastering regex can significantly broaden your data cleaning and preprocessing capabilities. The `stringr` package supports regex directly in its functions:

```r
# Extracting all words starting with 'b'
words_with_b <- str_extract_all(text, "\\bb\\w+")
print(words_with_b)
```

This code snippet uses the regex pattern `\\bb\\w+` to find all occurrences of words starting with the letter 'b'. The double backslash (`\\`) is used to escape special characters in R strings.

Text Mining Basics

Text mining involves extracting meaningful information from text data. This process often starts with text cleaning and preprocessing, which can include tasks such as removing punctuation, converting text to lowercase, or removing stopwords (common words that are usually filtered out). The `stringr` package can be employed for these preprocessing steps:

```r
# Removing punctuation
clean_text <- str_remove_all(text, "[[:punct:]]")
print(clean_text)
# Converting to lowercase
lower_text <- str_to_lower(clean_text)
print(lower_text)
```

Sentiment Analysis

Sentiment analysis is a technique used to determine the emotional tone behind a body of text. This is a common application of text mining that can be useful in various domains, such as social media monitoring, customer feedback, and market research. While `stringr` helps with the preprocessing of text for sentiment analysis, specific R packages like `syuzhet` or `tidytext` offer tools to perform the analysis itself:

```r
library(syuzhet)
sentiments <- get_sentiment(lower_text)
print(sentiments)
```

This simple example demonstrates how to obtain sentiment scores for the preprocessed text. Positive scores indicate positive sentiment, while negative scores indicate negative sentiment.

Text Classification

Text classification involves categorizing text into predefined groups. For example, classifying emails into 'spam' or 'non-spam'. This task often requires more advanced techniques, including machine learning models. The preprocessing of text data, as facilitated by `stringr`, is a crucial step before applying any classification algorithms.

In conclusion, working with text data in R using the `stringr` package and understanding regular expressions can significantly enhance your data analysis skills. From cleaning and preprocessing text to performing sentiment analysis and text classification, these tools provide a foundation for deeper insights into unstructured text data. As you continue to explore the capabilities of R in text data analysis, remember that practice is key to mastering these techniques.

String Manipulation with stringr

Building upon our exploration of **stringr** for effective text manipulation, let's delve into more advanced functionalities that can significantly streamline your data analysis workflow. **Stringr** not only simplifies common string operations but also introduces powerful capabilities for pattern recognition and string replacement, which are essential for cleaning and preparing text data for analysis.

Pattern Matching and Replacement

One of the most frequent tasks in text data analysis involves identifying and replacing patterns within strings. The `str_replace()` and `str_replace_all()` functions are invaluable tools for this purpose. While `str_replace()` replaces the first instance of a pattern, `str_replace_all()` targets all occurrences. Consider a scenario where you need to anonymize email addresses in a dataset:

```r
emails <- c("user1@example.com", "user2@example.com")
anonymized_emails <- str_replace_all(emails, "@example.com",
"@anonymous.com")
print(anonymized_emails)
```

This code snippet demonstrates how to replace the domain of email addresses to protect user privacy. Such operations are crucial when preparing data for public sharing or analysis.

Splitting Strings

Another common requirement is splitting a string into multiple parts based on a delimiter. The `str_split()` function divides a string into a list of strings using a specified separator. This function is particularly useful when working with complex data formats:

```r
record <- "John Doe, 30, New York"
fields <- str_split(record, ", ")
print(fields)
```

Here, `str_split()` is used to separate a record into its constituent parts, such as name, age, and location. Splitting strings facilitates the extraction of specific data elements for further analysis or visualization.

Trimming Whitespace

Whitespace management is a critical aspect of text preprocessing. Extraneous spaces can lead to inaccuracies in data analysis, especially when comparing or categorizing text. The `str_trim()` function removes leading and trailing whitespace from a string, ensuring consistency across your dataset:

```r
messy_string <- "    R Programming     "
```

```r
clean_string <- str_trim(messy_string)
print(clean_string)
```

Trimming whitespace is a simple yet effective step in data cleaning, enhancing the accuracy of your analysis outcomes.

Working with Case

Text data often varies in case, which can affect sorting, searching, and matching operations. The `str_to_upper()`, `str_to_lower()`, and `str_to_title()` functions allow you to standardize the case of your text data:

```r
r
original_text <- "r programming is fun"
upper_text <- str_to_upper(original_text)
lower_text <- str_to_lower(original_text)
title_text <- str_to_title(original_text)
print(upper_text)
print(lower_text)
print(title_text)
```

Converting text to a uniform case is essential for consistent data analysis, especially when dealing with user-generated content that may not follow a standard format.

Extracting Substrings

The `str_sub()` function enables the extraction of substrings from a string, based on start and end positions. This functionality is crucial when you need to isolate specific segments of text for analysis:

```r
r
full_text <- "Data analysis with R"
sub_text <- str_sub(full_text, 1, 4)
print(sub_text)
```

Extracting substrings is particularly useful when working with structured text data, such as log files or coded entries, where specific information is located at fixed positions within each record.

By mastering these advanced **stringr** functions, you can significantly enhance your text data preprocessing and analysis capabilities. Efficient string manipulation not only streamlines your workflow but also ensures that your data analysis is based on clean, consistent, and meaningful text data. As you continue to work with **stringr**, remember that the key to effective text data analysis lies in understanding the specific needs of your dataset and applying the appropriate string manipulation techniques to meet those needs.

Regular Expressions

Regular expressions, often abbreviated as **regex**, are sequences of characters that define a search pattern, primarily used for string matching and manipulation. In R, regular expressions allow you to perform complex text processing tasks with just a few lines of code. Understanding how to construct and apply regex patterns can significantly enhance your ability to work with text data, enabling you to extract, replace, split, or remove specific portions of strings based on patterns rather than fixed characters.

To start working with regular expressions in R, you'll often use functions from the `stringr` package, which integrates seamlessly with regex. The `str_detect()` function, for example, checks if a string contains a specified pattern:

```r
library(stringr)
text <- "Data analysis in R is exciting."
pattern <- "analysis"
str_detect(text, pattern)
```

This will return `TRUE` because the pattern "analysis" is found within the text. Regular expressions go beyond simple keyword searches, allowing for the specification of patterns that can match a wide range of text strings. For instance, to find any word that starts with "ex":

```r
```

```r
words_with_ex <- str_extract_all(text, "\\bex\\w+")
print(words_with_ex)
```

The pattern \\bex\\w+ is a regular expression where \\b denotes a word boundary, ex is the literal characters we're looking for, and \\w+ matches one or more word characters (letters, digits, or underscores) that follow. This pattern effectively extracts words that start with "ex", such as "exciting".

Regular expressions can also be used to replace parts of a string. The str_replace_all() function, for example, can be used to replace all occurrences of a pattern with a new string:

```r
replaced_text <- str_replace_all(text, "\\bis\\b", "can be")
print(replaced_text)
```

In this example, \\bis\\b matches the whole word "is", and it's replaced with "can be", demonstrating how regex can be used to modify text based on pattern matching.

When working with more complex text data, you might need to extract numbers, special characters, or formatted text like dates. Regular expressions make these tasks manageable. For example, to extract all numbers from a string:

```r
text_with_numbers <- "The event will take place on 24th June 2023."
numbers <- str_extract_all(text_with_numbers, "\\d+")
print(numbers)
```

The pattern \\d+ matches one or more digits, extracting "24" and "2023" from the text. This capability is particularly useful for cleaning and preprocessing text data before analysis.

Regular expressions can also facilitate the splitting of strings into components. The str_split() function can use a regex pattern as the delimiter:

```r
sentence <- "R,Python,Java"
```

```
languages <- str_split(sentence, ",")
print(languages)
```

Here, the comma , serves as a simple pattern to split the string into individual programming languages. For more complex scenarios, regex allows you to specify patterns that include optional characters, alternation, or specific character sets to match against.

In summary, mastering regular expressions in R opens up a vast array of possibilities for text data manipulation and analysis. Whether you're cleaning data, extracting information, or performing text transformations, regex provides a powerful toolset that, when combined with R's string manipulation functions, can handle virtually any text processing task you encounter. As you become more familiar with regular expressions, you'll find that tasks that once seemed tedious or complex can be accomplished quickly and efficiently, enhancing both your productivity and the depth of your data analysis projects.

Text Mining Basics

Text mining, often referred to as text analytics, is a process of deriving meaningful information from natural language text. In R, this involves a variety of techniques and tools, primarily focusing on the manipulation and analysis of unstructured text data. The stringr package is a powerful tool for string operations, but for text mining, we often rely on the tm (Text Mining) package, which provides a framework for text mining applications within R.

To start with text mining in R, you first need to install and load the tm package. You can do this by running:

```R
install.packages("tm")
library(tm)
```

Once the package is loaded, the first step in text mining is usually to create a text corpus. A corpus is a collection of text documents, and in tm, this is represented by the Corpus object. You can create a corpus from a vector of texts, a directory of text files, or even from a data frame. For simplicity, let's create a corpus from a vector of texts:

```R
texts <- c("Text mining is awesome", "R makes text mining easy",
"We can extract useful information from text")
corpus <- Corpus(VectorSource(texts))
```

After creating a corpus, preprocessing is an essential step. This includes transforming the text to lower case, removing punctuation, stopwords (common words that do not carry much meaning, like "the", "is", etc.), and stemming (reducing words to their root form). These steps help in reducing the complexity of the text data and focus on the meaningful content. Here's how you can perform these preprocessing steps in R:

```R
corpus <- tm_map(corpus, content_transformer(tolower))
corpus <- tm_map(corpus, removePunctuation)
corpus <- tm_map(corpus, removeWords, stopwords("english"))
corpus <- tm_map(corpus, stemDocument)
```

After preprocessing, the next step is to convert the text data into a matrix of document-term frequencies, often called a Document-Term Matrix (DTM). This matrix represents the frequency of terms that occur in the collection of documents. In tm, you can create a DTM using the DocumentTermMatrix function:

```R
dtm <- DocumentTermMatrix(corpus)
```

Analyzing the DTM can reveal patterns and trends in the text data. For example, finding the most frequently occurring terms can be done by summing across the matrix's columns:

```R
freq <- colSums(as.matrix(dtm))
ord <- order(freq, decreasing = TRUE)
freq[ord]
```

This will give you a list of terms sorted by their frequency across the corpus, which can be very insightful for understanding the main topics or themes within the text data.

Text mining is a vast field, and R provides a comprehensive ecosystem for text analysis, including packages for sentiment analysis, topic modeling, and more. The `tm` package is just the starting point, and as you become more comfortable with text mining basics, you can explore other packages like `wordcloud` for generating word clouds, `topicmodels` for Latent Dirichlet Allocation (LDA), and `syuzhet` for sentiment analysis. Each of these tools opens new possibilities for extracting insights from text data, enabling you to transform unstructured text into structured, actionable information.

Sentiment Analysis

Sentiment analysis, often referred to as opinion mining, is a powerful text mining technique used to determine the emotional tone behind a body of text. This is a crucial step in understanding the attitudes, opinions, and emotions expressed in the online content, reviews, or feedback. In R, several packages facilitate sentiment analysis, but one of the most accessible and widely used is the `syuzhet` package. This package offers a straightforward approach to extract sentiment from textual data, allowing us to gauge public opinion about a particular topic or product.

To begin with sentiment analysis in R using the `syuzhet` package, you first need to install and load it into your R environment:

R

```
install.packages("syuzhet")
library(syuzhet)
```

Once the package is loaded, you can start analyzing the sentiment of texts. The `syuzhet` package provides multiple methods to extract sentiment, but one of the simplest ways is to use the `get_sentiment` function. This function calculates sentiment scores using various sentiment dictionaries. For a basic analysis, you might start with the default method, which is based on the "syuzhet" dictionary:

R

```
text <- "R makes data analysis so much easier and more fun!"
sentiment_score <- get_sentiment(text)
print(sentiment_score)
```

This code snippet will return a sentiment score indicating the overall emotional tone of the text. Positive scores indicate positive sentiment, while negative scores indicate negative sentiment. Scores close to zero can be considered neutral.

For a more nuanced analysis, you might be interested in how the sentiment varies throughout a text. The `get_nrc_sentiment` function breaks down the text into ten different emotions: anger, anticipation, disgust, fear, joy, sadness, surprise, trust, negative, and positive. This can be particularly useful for analyzing longer texts or comparing the emotional content of different documents:

```R
sentiment_by_emotion <- get_nrc_sentiment(text)
print(sentiment_by_emotion)
```

This function returns a data frame where each row represents the text and each column an emotion, with the values indicating the presence of each emotion in the text.

For those working with larger datasets or multiple texts, sentiment analysis can be applied to each text in a corpus using the `sapply` or `lapply` functions. Suppose you have a vector of texts; you can easily calculate the sentiment for each text as follows:

```R
texts <- c("I love using R for data analysis.", "R can be
frustrating at times.", "Data visualization in R is fantastic.")
sentiment_scores <- sapply(texts, get_sentiment)
print(sentiment_scores)
```

This approach allows for batch processing of texts, making it efficient to analyze sentiment across a large collection of documents.

Sentiment analysis in R is not limited to English. The `syuzhet` package supports multiple languages, allowing for a broad application of sentiment analysis across different linguistic datasets. However, the accuracy and availability of sentiment dictionaries may vary by language, so it's important to consider this when analyzing texts in languages other than English.

In practice, sentiment analysis is a powerful tool for data scientists, marketers, and researchers interested in gauging public opinion, monitoring brand reputation, or understanding customer feedback. By leveraging R and its packages for sentiment analysis, you can uncover valuable insights from textual data, transforming unstructured text into structured, actionable information. Whether analyzing a single review or thousands of social media posts, sentiment analysis provides a window into the emotions and opinions expressed in text, offering a deeper understanding of the data at hand.

Text Classification

Building on the foundation of sentiment analysis, **text classification** stands as a pivotal technique in text mining, enabling the categorization of textual data into predefined groups or classes. This process is instrumental in organizing, understanding, and extracting meaningful information from vast amounts of text data. In R, the task of text classification can be approached through various packages and functions, with the `caret` package being notably versatile for creating predictive models, including those needed for classifying text.

To embark on text classification, one must first ensure the text data is preprocessed, as discussed in previous sections. Following preprocessing, the creation of a Document-Term Matrix (DTM) or a Term Frequency-Inverse Document Frequency (TF-IDF) matrix is crucial. The TF-IDF matrix is particularly beneficial for text classification as it reflects how important a word is to a document in a collection, thus helping in differentiating documents more effectively than simple term frequencies.

```R
library(tm)
# Assuming 'corpus' is your preprocessed text corpus
dtm <- DocumentTermMatrix(corpus)
tfidf <- weightTfIdf(dtm)
```

After preparing your data, the next step involves splitting it into training and testing sets to evaluate the performance of your classification model accurately. The `caret` package provides functions to streamline this process.

```R
library(caret)
set.seed(123) # For reproducibility
# Assuming 'tfidf' is your TF-IDF matrix and 'labels' are your class labels
data <- as.data.frame(as.matrix(tfidf))
```

```
data$label <- labels # Add labels to your data frame
inTrain <- createDataPartition(data$label, p = 0.7, list = FALSE)
training <- data[inTrain,]
testing <- data[-inTrain,]
```

With your data prepared and split, you can now train a model for text classification. The caret package supports various machine learning algorithms; for simplicity, we'll use a Naive Bayes classifier, which is often effective for text data due to its assumption of independence among the features.

R
```
model <- train(label ~ ., data = training, method = "naive_bayes")
```

After training the model, you can use it to predict the classes of new, unseen texts (represented in your testing set). The performance of your model can be assessed using metrics such as accuracy, precision, recall, and F1 score, which caret can calculate for you.

R
```
predictions <- predict(model, testing)
confusionMatrix(predictions, testing$label)
```

This process illustrates a basic workflow for text classification in R, from preprocessing text data to training and evaluating a model. The versatility of R's packages like tm for text mining and caret for machine learning modeling opens up a wide array of possibilities for text classification tasks. Whether categorizing emails into spam and non-spam, organizing documents by topics, or identifying sentiment in social media posts, text classification serves as a powerful tool in the data scientist's arsenal, enabling the extraction of valuable insights from textual data.

As you delve deeper into text classification, exploring different algorithms and tuning model parameters can significantly enhance your model's performance. Additionally, considering the context and nuances of your specific text data is crucial in choosing the right preprocessing steps and features to include in your model. With practice and experimentation, text classification in R can become an invaluable skill in your data analysis toolkit, allowing you to uncover patterns and insights in textual data that would otherwise remain hidden.

CHAPTER 8

Advanced Topics in R

Building on the foundation of sentiment analysis, **text classification** stands as a pivotal technique in text mining, enabling the categorization of textual data into predefined groups or classes. This process is instrumental in organizing, understanding, and extracting meaningful information from vast amounts of text data. In R, the task of text classification can be approached through various packages and functions, with the `caret` package being notably versatile for creating predictive models, including those needed for classifying text.

To embark on text classification, one must first ensure the text data is preprocessed, as discussed in previous sections. Following preprocessing, the creation of a Document-Term Matrix (DTM) or a Term Frequency-Inverse Document Frequency (TF-IDF) matrix is crucial. The TF-IDF matrix is particularly beneficial for text classification as it reflects how important a word is to a document in a collection, thus helping in differentiating documents more effectively than simple term frequencies.

```R
library(tm)
# Assuming 'corpus' is your preprocessed text corpus
dtm <- DocumentTermMatrix(corpus)
tfidf <- weightTfIdf(dtm)
```

After preparing your data, the next step involves splitting it into training and testing sets to evaluate the performance of your classification model accurately. The `caret` package provides functions to streamline this process.

```R
R
library(caret)
set.seed(123) # For reproducibility
# Assuming 'tfidf' is your TF-IDF matrix and 'labels' are your
class labels
data <- as.data.frame(as.matrix(tfidf))
data$label <- labels # Add labels to your data frame
inTrain <- createDataPartition(data$label, p = 0.7, list = FALSE)
training <- data[inTrain,]
testing <- data[-inTrain,]
```

With your data prepared and split, you can now train a model for text classification. The `caret` package supports various machine learning algorithms; for simplicity, we'll use a Naive Bayes classifier, which is often effective for text data due to its assumption of independence among the features.

```R
R
model <- train(label ~ ., data = training, method = "naive_bayes")
```

After training the model, you can use it to predict the classes of new, unseen texts (represented in your testing set). The performance of your model can be assessed using metrics such as accuracy, precision, recall, and F1 score, which `caret` can calculate for you.

```R
R
predictions <- predict(model, testing)
confusionMatrix(predictions, testing$label)
```

This process illustrates a basic workflow for text classification in R, from preprocessing text data to training and evaluating a model. The versatility of R's packages like `tm` for text mining and `caret` for machine learning modeling opens up a wide array of possibilities for text classification tasks. Whether categorizing emails into spam and non-spam, organizing documents by topics, or identifying sentiment in social media posts, text classification serves as a powerful tool in the data scientist's arsenal, enabling the extraction of valuable insights from textual data.

For those looking to delve deeper into the nuances of text classification, feature engineering plays a critical role in enhancing model performance. Feature engineering involves creating new input features from your existing data, aiming to highlight important aspects that the model might otherwise overlook. In the context of text classification, this could involve the extraction of n-grams, which are contiguous sequences of n items from a given sample of text. N-grams help capture context and semantics, potentially improving the model's ability to differentiate between classes.

R

```r
# Example of extracting bigrams (2-grams) from text data
library(text2vec)
texts <- c("R is great for data analysis", "Data science with R is fun")
it <- itoken(texts, tokenizer = word_tokenizer, ids = c("doc1", "doc2"))
vectorizer <- vocab_vectorizer(vocabulary = create_vocabulary(it))
dtm <- create_dtm(it, vectorizer)
bigram_vectorizer <- vocab_vectorizer(create_vocabulary(it, ngram = c(ngram_min = 2, ngram_max = 2)))
bigram_dtm <- create_dtm(it, bigram_vectorizer)
```

In addition to n-grams, term frequency-inverse document frequency (TF-IDF) transformations are crucial for highlighting words that are frequent in a document but not across documents. This helps in emphasizing terms that are uniquely significant to specific documents, further refining the model's accuracy.

Once you've engineered your features and trained your model, interpreting the model's predictions is the next step. Understanding why your model has made certain classifications is crucial for validating its reliability and for providing insights that can guide further refinement. Techniques such as analyzing the model's feature importances or applying model-agnostic interpretation methods can shed light on the decision-making process of your classifier.

R

```r
# Example of examining feature importance in a Naive Bayes model
if (requireNamespace("caret", quietly = TRUE)) {
```

```
    varImp(model, scale = FALSE)
}
```

Beyond Naive Bayes, exploring other algorithms like Support Vector Machines (SVM), Random Forests, or even deep learning models can offer improvements in classification performance. Each algorithm comes with its own set of strengths and considerations, making it important to experiment with various approaches to find the best fit for your specific text classification challenge.

```R
# Example of training a SVM model
svm_model <- train(label ~ ., data = training, method =
"svmRadial")
```

Finally, continuous evaluation and iteration are key. Text classification is not a one-time process but rather an ongoing cycle of refining your model based on new data, feedback, and evolving requirements. Regularly updating your model with fresh data, re-evaluating its performance, and tweaking your feature engineering and modeling approaches are essential practices for maintaining high accuracy and relevance in your text classification efforts.

By embracing these advanced strategies and continuously seeking to understand and improve your model, you can unlock deeper insights from your text data, making your text classification endeavors not only more accurate but also more impactful. Whether you're analyzing customer feedback, moderating content, or categorizing news articles, the power of text classification in R is a formidable tool in your data analysis arsenal, enabling you to derive meaningful patterns and trends from complex textual datasets.

Working with Big Data in R

Handling big data in R requires a strategic approach to efficiently process and analyze large datasets that may not fit into the memory of a standard computer. One of the key strategies involves the use of the bigmemory package, which allows for the creation, storage, access, and manipulation of massive matrices. The bigmemory package provides a pointer to data that is stored on disk, enabling operations on datasets that exceed the available RAM.

To begin working with `bigmemory`, you first need to install and load the package:

```R
install.packages("bigmemory")
library(bigmemory)
```

After loading the package, you can create a big matrix from an existing data frame or matrix using the `as.big.matrix` function. This function converts your data into a format that `bigmemory` can work with, allowing for efficient data manipulation and analysis.

```R
data_matrix <- matrix(rnorm(1000000), nrow = 1000)
big_matrix <- as.big.matrix(data_matrix)
```

The `big.matrix` object now points to a dataset that is stored on disk, rather than in RAM, which significantly reduces the memory overhead for your R session. This is particularly useful when dealing with large datasets that need to be processed or analyzed in chunks.

For data analysis, the `bigmemory` package integrates with other packages such as `biganalytics` and `bigalgebra` for statistical analysis and algebraic operations on `big.matrix` objects. For instance, you can perform row-wise and column-wise operations, compute summary statistics, and even apply machine learning algorithms to your big data.

Another powerful package for working with big data in R is `ff`. The `ff` package offers data structures that are stored on disk but behave almost as if they were in RAM, providing transparent access to very large datasets. Similar to `bigmemory`, `ff` enables operations on datasets that are larger than the available memory.

To use `ff`, start by installing and loading the package:

```R
install.packages("ff")
library(ff)
```

You can then create `ff` objects, which are essentially pointers to data files on disk. These objects can be manipulated in a manner similar to in-memory R objects, but without the associated memory limitations.

```R
ff_vector <- ff(runif(1000000))
ff_matrix <- ffmatrix(runif(10000000), ncol = 100)
```

The `ff` package also supports a wide range of operations, including subsetting, merging, and sorting, making it a versatile tool for big data analysis in R.

For truly large-scale data analysis, the `data.table` package can be an excellent choice. It extends the `data.frame` to offer fast aggregation of large datasets, fast ordered joins, and other essential data manipulation capabilities. The syntax and functionality of `data.table` make it highly efficient for operations on large datasets.

```R
install.packages("data.table")
library(data.table)
DT <- data.table(x = runif(10000000), y = rep(1:100, each = 100000))
```

With `data.table`, operations that would typically be computationally intensive and time-consuming on large datasets can be executed quickly and with minimal coding effort.

In summary, working with big data in R is facilitated by a range of packages designed to efficiently handle and analyze datasets that exceed the memory capacity of standard computing environments. By leveraging `bigmemory`, `ff`, and `data.table`, among others, you can perform complex data analysis tasks on large datasets with relative ease. These tools are essential for data scientists and analysts who regularly work with big data, providing the means to extract meaningful insights from large and complex datasets.

R Markdown and Reporting

R Markdown is an essential tool for data analysis and reporting in R, allowing users to combine narrative, code, and output in a single document. This powerful feature facilitates reproducible research and dynamic report generation, making it easier to share insights with others. To get started with R Markdown, you first need to install the necessary packages. The `rmarkdown` package can be installed from CRAN, and if you're using

RStudio, it integrates seamlessly with the IDE, providing an easy-to-use interface for creating and managing R Markdown documents.

```R
install.packages("rmarkdown")
```

Once installed, you can create a new R Markdown document in RStudio by going to File > New File > R Markdown. This will open a dialog where you can choose the document type (HTML, PDF, or Word) and specify other options such as the title and author. The default template provides a basic structure for your document, including sections for the title, author, date, and various headers.

An R Markdown document is composed of two main types of content: text and code chunks. Text is written in Markdown, a lightweight markup language that allows you to format text using simple syntax. For example, you can create headers using #, bold text with **, and lists with - or *. Code chunks, on the other hand, are enclosed in triple backticks and include {r} at the beginning to indicate that they contain R code. Within these chunks, you can write R code that will be executed when the document is rendered. The output of the code, including plots, can be automatically included in the final document.

```markdown
---
title: "My First R Markdown Report"
author: "Jane Doe"
date: "2023-03-15"
output: html_document
---

This is an R Markdown document. Markdown is a simple formatting
syntax for authoring HTML, PDF, and MS Word documents. For more
details on using R Markdown see <http://rmarkdown.rstudio.com>.

## R Code

Here is an example of R code in an R Markdown document:

{r cars}

summary(cars)
```

Plot

You can also embed plots. For example:

```
{r pressure, echo=FALSE}
```

```
plot(pressure)
```

To render your document into a finished product, you can click the "Knit" button in RStudio, which will compile the document into the specified format (HTML, PDF, or Word). The `knitr` package is used behind the scenes to execute the R code chunks and embed the results into the document. The `pandoc` tool is then used to convert the document into the desired output format.

R Markdown documents can be customized in various ways using YAML metadata at the top of the document. This metadata section allows you to specify document settings such as the output format, document title, author, and date. You can also include other settings like CSS styles for HTML documents, LaTeX packages for PDF documents, and reference docx templates for Word documents.

R Markdown is not limited to simple reports; it can also be used to create presentations, dashboards, and even interactive web applications with Shiny. This versatility makes it an invaluable tool for data scientists and analysts who need to communicate their findings effectively.

For more advanced users, R Markdown supports parameterized reports, which allow you to create a single template that can generate different reports based on input parameters. This feature is particularly useful for generating customized reports for different audiences or datasets.

In summary, R Markdown provides a powerful, flexible, and reproducible way to create dynamic documents that combine code, output, and narrative. Whether you're writing a simple analysis report, a thesis, or a complex interactive dashboard, R Markdown can help you communicate your findings clearly and effectively.

Dynamic Reporting

Dynamic reporting in R leverages the power of R Markdown to create interactive and dynamic documents, presentations, and dashboards. This capability transforms static analysis into engaging, live documents that can update with new data or user input. Here, we delve into how to enhance your R Markdown documents to create dynamic reports.

To begin, ensure you have the `rmarkdown` and `knitr` packages installed and loaded in your R environment. These packages are essential for knitting R Markdown documents into various formats like HTML, PDF, and Word.

```r
install.packages(c("rmarkdown", "knitr"))
library(rmarkdown)
library(knitr)
```

Parameterized Reports

Parameterized reports allow you to create a single R Markdown document that can generate different outputs based on parameters. This is particularly useful for reports that need to be generated for different departments, geographical regions, or time periods.

To create a parameterized report, you add a `params` field to the YAML header of your R Markdown document. Here's an example:

```yaml
---
title: "Sales Report"
output: html_document
params:
  region: "North America"
---
```

In your R Markdown document, you can access the parameter using `params$region`. This allows you to dynamically change the content of the report based on the parameter value.

Interactive Documents with Shiny

Integrating Shiny apps into R Markdown documents elevates the interactivity of your reports. Shiny allows users to interact with your R Markdown document in real-time, changing inputs and seeing the output update immediately.

To create an interactive document, you'll need to use the `runtime: shiny` option in the YAML header:

```yaml
---
title: "Interactive Analysis"
output: html_document
runtime: shiny
---
```

Within the document, you can add Shiny components using R code chunks. For example, to add a slider input and a plot that updates based on the slider value:

```r
inputPanel(
  sliderInput("bins", "Number of Bins:", min = 1, max = 50, value =
30)
)
renderPlot({
  x <- faithful$eruptions
  bins <- seq(min(x), max(x), length.out = input$bins + 1)
  hist(x, breaks = bins, col = 'darkgray', border = 'white')
})
```

Dynamic Visualization

Dynamic reporting is not just about changing text or data; it's also about dynamic visualizations. The ggplot2 package, combined with plotly, can turn static plots into interactive visualizations.

First, create a ggplot object:

```r
library(ggplot2)
p <- ggplot(data = mtcars, aes(x = wt, y = mpg)) + geom_point()
```

Then, convert it to a plotly object for interactivity:

```r
library(plotly)
ggplotly(p)
```

This approach allows users to hover over points to see more information, zoom in and out, and pan across the plot, making the data exploration more interactive and engaging.

Embedding External Applications

Dynamic reports can also include content from external sources or applications. For instance, embedding a Google Sheets document or an interactive Tableau dashboard directly into an R Markdown document. This is achieved using the `iframe` HTML tag within an R Markdown code chunk:

```r
htmltools::tags$iframe(src = "https://yourdashboardlink", width =
"100%", height = "400")
```

By incorporating these dynamic reporting techniques, your R Markdown documents can become more interactive, personalized, and engaging. Whether it's through parameterized reports, Shiny applications, dynamic visualizations, or embedding external content, the possibilities are vast, allowing you to tailor your reports to meet the evolving needs of your audience.

Creating Presentations

Creating presentations with R Markdown extends the dynamic and interactive capabilities of your reports into the realm of engaging, visually appealing slideshows. This powerful feature allows you to present your data analysis results in a structured and accessible format, suitable for both academic and professional settings.

To start crafting your presentation, you'll need to specify the output format in the YAML header of your R Markdown document. For presentations, `ioslides_presentation` or `slidy_presentation` are popular choices due to their simplicity and web browser compatibility:

```yaml
---
```

```
title: "My Data Analysis Presentation"
author: "Your Name"
date: "2023-03-15"
output: ioslides_presentation
---
```

With the output format set, you can begin organizing your content into slides. Each slide is created using a new section header. For example, to create a title slide followed by a slide with a plot, your R Markdown might look like this:

```markdown
# My Data Analysis Presentation
## Introduction
Here's where you can introduce the topic of your presentation.
## Data Visualization
```

```{r, echo=FALSE}
library(ggplot2)

ggplot(data = mtcars, aes(x = wt, y = mpg)) + geom_point()
```

Slide Transitions and Layouts: Customize the appearance of your slides and transitions between them by using specific options in the YAML header or directly in your slides. For instance, adding `incremental: true` under a slide header will reveal bullet points one at a time.

Embedding Code and Results: Just like in other R Markdown documents, you can embed R code chunks and display their results directly in your slides. This is ideal for live demonstrations of data analysis techniques or for showcasing the results of your analysis.

Including Images and Videos: Enhance your presentation by including relevant images, videos, or even interactive Shiny applications. Use the Markdown syntax for images and HTML tags for videos. For Shiny applications, you'll need to host the app online and embed it using an iframe.

```html
html
!<a href="path/to/image.png">Alt text for an image</a>
<video controls>
  <source src="path/to/video.mp4" type="video/mp4">
Your browser does not support the video tag.
</video>
```

Interactive Polls and Quizzes: Engage your audience with interactive polls or quizzes. Tools like `polleverywhere.com` can be integrated into your slides, allowing for real-time audience participation and feedback.

Sharing Your Presentation: Once your presentation is ready, you can share it by hosting the HTML file on a web server or using services like GitHub Pages. Alternatively, RStudio Connect is a professional publishing platform that supports hosting for R Markdown documents, including presentations.

By leveraging the capabilities of R Markdown for creating presentations, you can effectively communicate your data analysis findings in a structured and visually appealing format. This approach not only enhances the delivery of your content but also engages your audience with interactive elements and live demonstrations.

Building R Packages

Building R packages is an essential skill for any R user who wishes to share their functions, data, and research with others in a structured and accessible manner. The process involves several key steps: setting up the package structure, writing functions, documenting the package, and finally, testing and distributing it.

Setting Up the Package Structure

The first step in creating an R package is to establish a proper package structure. This can be efficiently done using the `usethis` and `devtools` packages. Start by creating a new package directory with the `create_package()` function from the `usethis` package:

```r
r
usethis::create_package("path/to/yourPackageName")
```

This function creates a new directory containing the basic structure of an R package, including folders for R scripts, documentation, and tests.

Writing Functions

The core of any R package is its functions. Each function you plan to include in your package should be placed in its own file within the R/ directory. Ensure that your functions are well-written, following best practices for coding in R, and include clear, concise comments to explain the purpose and functionality of each function.

Documenting the Package

Documentation is crucial for any package. It helps users understand how to use your functions and what each argument does. The roxygen2 package simplifies the documentation process in R. By adding special roxygen comments above your function definitions, you can document your functions directly within your R scripts. Running devtools::document() then processes these comments into the man/ directory, containing the .Rd (R documentation) files.

```r
#' Add together two numbers
#'
#' @param x A number.
#' @param y A number.
#' @return The sum of \code{x} and \code{y}.
#' @examples
#' add_numbers(1, 2)
add_numbers <- function(x, y) {
  return(x + y)
}
```

Testing Your Package

Before distributing your package, it's important to test its functions to ensure they work as expected. The testthat package provides a framework for writing and running tests in R. Create a tests/ directory in your package, and use testthat to write tests for each of your functions. Running devtools::test() executes these tests, helping you identify and fix any issues before release.

Distributing Your Package

Once your package is complete, you can distribute it in several ways. The most common method is through CRAN (The Comprehensive R Archive Network), which requires submitting your package for review. Alternatively, you can host your package on GitHub, allowing users to install it directly using

```
devtools::install_github("yourUsername/yourPackageName").
```

Remember, building an R package is not just about coding. It's about creating a tool that is useful, user-friendly, and well-documented. By following these steps and adhering to R's package development best practices, you can contribute valuable resources to the R community.

Interactive Web Applications with Shiny

Shiny is a powerful package in R that enables the creation of interactive web applications directly from R. This section will guide you through the process of building a basic Shiny app that demonstrates the dynamic interactivity Shiny offers. The app will allow users to input a range of numbers and visualize the distribution of those numbers in a histogram.

First, ensure you have Shiny installed and loaded in your R environment:

```r
install.packages("shiny")
library(shiny)
```

Building a Basic Shiny App

A Shiny app consists of two main components: a user interface (UI) and a server function. The UI defines the layout and appearance of your app, while the server function contains the instructions to build and modify the app based on user input.

1. Define the UI

Use the `fluidPage` function to create a flexible page layout that adjusts to the size of the user's screen. Inside `fluidPage`, use `titlePanel` to add a title to your app, `sidebarLayout` to add a sidebar for inputs, and `mainPanel` to display outputs.

```r
ui <- fluidPage(
  titlePanel("Interactive Histogram"),
  sidebarLayout(
    sidebarPanel(
      sliderInput("num", "Number of bins:",
                  min = 1,
                  max = 50,
                  value = 30)
    ),
    mainPanel(
      plotOutput("distPlot")
    )
  )
)
```

2. Define the Server Function

The server function takes input values from the UI, processes them, and returns the output to display in the UI. Use `renderPlot` to generate the histogram based on the number of bins specified by the user.

```r
server <- function(input, output) {
  output$distPlot <- renderPlot({
    x <- faithful$eruptions
    bins <- seq(min(x), max(x), length.out = input$num + 1)
    hist(x, breaks = bins, col = 'darkgray', border = 'white')
  })
}
```

3. Run the App

Use the `shinyApp` function to create and start the Shiny app by passing the UI and server components as arguments.

```r
   shinyApp(ui = ui, server = server)
```

When you run this code, a web browser will automatically open, displaying your interactive Shiny app. The slider in the sidebar allows users to adjust the number of bins in the histogram, and the main panel updates the histogram in real-time based on the slider's position.

Enhancing Your Shiny App

To further enhance your Shiny app, consider adding more input options for users, such as dropdown menus or text input fields, to control different aspects of the plot. Additionally, explore the `reactive` function to create reactive expressions that automatically update outputs when inputs change, making your app more efficient and responsive.

Shiny also supports advanced UI features like tabs and navigation bars, enabling the development of complex, multi-page applications. With these tools, you can create highly interactive and user-friendly web applications for data analysis and visualization, all within R.

By following these steps and exploring the extensive features of Shiny, you can transform your data analysis into interactive web applications that engage and inform users. Whether for educational purposes, data exploration, or presenting analysis results, Shiny apps offer a dynamic platform to visualize and interact with R data.

UI and Server Components

Building upon the foundational knowledge of Shiny for creating interactive web applications, it's crucial to delve deeper into the intricacies of **UI (User Interface)** and **Server Components**. These two elements are the backbone of any Shiny app, dictating how the app looks and operates. Understanding how to effectively design and implement these components is key to enhancing the user experience and functionality of your Shiny applications.

UI Components

The UI component in Shiny is responsible for the layout and appearance of the application. It's defined using a series of functions that specify what the user sees in the browser. The `fluidPage` function is often used as the container for the UI, providing a responsive layout that adapts to different screen sizes. Within `fluidPage`, you can incorporate various layout functions such as `sidebarLayout` for a sidebar and main panel configuration, or `tabsetPanel` for tabbed content.

```r
ui <- fluidPage(
  titlePanel("Your App Title"),
  sidebarLayout(
    sidebarPanel(
      # Input: Specify input elements here
    ),
    mainPanel(
      # Output: Display outputs here
    )
  )
)
```

Customizing the UI: To tailor the appearance of your app, Shiny offers a range of functions for adding widgets, text, images, and more. For instance, `sliderInput` creates a slider for numeric input, while `plotOutput` reserves space for displaying plots. The `theme` argument in `fluidPage` or specific functions like `tags$head` can be used to include custom CSS for further customization.

Server Components

The server component contains the server logic of your Shiny app. It's a function that takes input values from the UI, processes them, and returns the output to be displayed. The server function uses **reactive programming** principles, allowing it to automatically update outputs in response to user inputs.

```r
```

```
server <- function(input, output) {
  output$yourOutputID <- renderPlot({
    # Your data processing and plotting code here
  })
}
```

Reactive Expressions: For more complex applications, you might need to perform some calculations or data processing based on user input before generating the output. Reactive expressions (reactive) are used for this purpose. They monitor changes in their dependencies (input values or other reactive expressions) and only re-execute when necessary, improving the app's efficiency.

r
```
reactiveData <- reactive({
  # Data processing code that responds to user input
})
```

You can then use reactiveData() as if it were a regular R object in your server logic to generate outputs.

Integrating UI and Server Components

To bring your Shiny app to life, the UI and server components are combined using the shinyApp function. This function takes the UI and server definitions as arguments and creates the interactive web application.

r
```
shinyApp(ui = ui, server = server)
```

Advanced UI-Server Interaction: For advanced applications, you might need more sophisticated communication between the UI and server. Shiny provides functions like updateSliderInput to programmatically change the UI from the server side based on certain conditions or user actions. Similarly, observeEvent and eventReactive are powerful for triggering reactive expressions or actions based on specific events or inputs.

By mastering the UI and server components of Shiny, you can create highly interactive and user-friendly web applications. These applications can serve a wide range of purposes, from simple data visualizations to complex data analysis tools, all accessible through a web browser. Remember, the key to a successful Shiny app lies in the thoughtful integration of its UI and server components, ensuring a seamless and engaging user experience.

Deploying Shiny Apps

Deploying Shiny apps is the final step in sharing your interactive web applications with a broader audience. This process involves moving your application from a local development environment to a server where it can be accessed by users through the internet. There are several platforms and strategies for deploying Shiny apps, each with its own set of features and considerations. The most common methods include ShinyApps.io, RStudio Connect, and self-hosting with a Shiny Server.

ShinyApps.io is a popular choice for deploying Shiny apps due to its simplicity and integration with RStudio. It's a platform-as-a-service (PaaS) offering that allows you to deploy apps directly from RStudio IDE with just a few clicks. To get started, you'll need to install the rsconnect package:

```r
install.packages("rsconnect")
```

After installing the package, you can deploy your app to ShinyApps.io by using the rsconnect::deployApp() function. Before deploying, you'll need to set up an account on ShinyApps.io and configure your RStudio to connect to your account. The rsconnect package provides functions to authenticate and save your credentials securely.

```r
rsconnect::setAccountInfo(name="<account_name>", token="<account_token>", secret="<secret>")
```

Once your account is configured, deploying your app is as simple as navigating to your app's directory in RStudio and running:

```r
rsconnect::deployApp()
```

This command uploads your app's files to ShinyApps.io and provides you with a URL to access your app. ShinyApps.io handles the hosting and scaling of your app, making it accessible to users worldwide without the need for you to manage a server.

RStudio Connect is a more comprehensive platform designed for enterprise use. It supports not only Shiny applications but also R Markdown documents, Plumber APIs, and more. RStudio Connect offers more control over who can access your apps and how they are deployed, making it suitable for sensitive or proprietary applications. Deploying to RStudio Connect is similar to deploying to ShinyApps.io but requires an RStudio Connect server.

For those who prefer or require full control over their hosting environment, **self-hosting with Shiny Server** is an option. Shiny Server is an open-source server software that you can install on your own Linux server. It allows you to host multiple Shiny applications and manage user access. Installing Shiny Server involves downloading and configuring the software on your server, and then deploying your apps by copying them to a specific directory on the server.

```bash
sudo apt-get install gdebi-core
wget https://download3.rstudio.org/ubuntu-14.04/x86_64/shiny-server-1.5.16.958-amd64.deb
sudo gdebi shiny-server-1.5.16.958-amd64.deb
```

After installing Shiny Server, you can deploy your app by copying your app's directory to `/srv/shiny-server/`. You'll also need to configure the server settings to meet your needs, which can be done by editing the Shiny Server configuration file located at `/etc/shiny-server/shiny-server.conf`.

Deploying Shiny apps, whether through ShinyApps.io, RStudio Connect, or self-hosting with Shiny Server, involves considerations around accessibility, security, and resource management. Each method offers different levels of control and ease of use, allowing you to choose the best approach based on your specific needs and resources. Regardless of the deployment method chosen, the end goal is the same: to make your interactive Shiny applications available to users, facilitating data exploration and visualization in a dynamic and engaging way.

CHAPTER 9

Practical Exercises in R

In this section, we'll dive into practical exercises designed to solidify your understanding of R and enhance your data analysis skills. These exercises are crafted to challenge and expand your knowledge, applying the concepts and techniques you've learned throughout this book. Let's start with **Data Import and Cleaning Exercises**. The ability to import and clean data efficiently is a cornerstone of effective data analysis. These exercises will test your skills in preparing raw data for analysis, a critical step before any meaningful insights can be drawn.

1. **Reading CSV Files**: Use the `read.csv()` function to import a CSV file into R. Once imported, explore the dataset using functions like `head()`, `tail()`, and `summary()` to get a feel for the data. For example:

```R
data <- read.csv("path/to/your/file.csv")
head(data)
```

2. **Handling Missing Values**: Identify missing values in your dataset using the `is.na()` function. Practice replacing these missing values with a mean or median value for the column, or consider removing rows with missing values entirely, depending on the context of your analysis. For instance:

```R
data$column[is.na(data$column)] <- mean(data$column, na.rm = TRUE)
```

3. **Data Type Conversion**: Convert the data types of columns as needed using functions like `as.numeric()`, `as.factor()`, and `as.Date()`. This is crucial for ensuring that your data is in the correct format for analysis. For example:

R

```
data$column <- as.numeric(data$column)
```

4. **Cleaning Text Data**: Utilize the `gsub()` function to clean text data, such as removing unwanted characters or formatting strings. This is particularly useful when dealing with data scraped from the web or imported from various text sources. For instance:

R

```
data$column <- gsub("[^a-zA-Z0-9 ]", "", data$column)
```

These exercises are designed to be both challenging and instructive, providing you with hands-on experience in data manipulation and preparation tasks that are common in data analysis workflows. As you work through these exercises, remember to refer back to the concepts and techniques discussed in earlier chapters, applying them as needed to solve the problems at hand.

Moving on to **Data Visualization Exercises**, mastering the art of presenting data is just as important as being able to analyze it. These exercises will help you practice creating compelling visualizations using `ggplot2` and `plotly`, enhancing your ability to communicate insights effectively.

1. **Creating Basic Plots with ggplot2**: Start by generating a simple scatter plot to visualize the relationship between two variables in your dataset. Use the `ggplot()` function along with `geom_point()`, and don't forget to label your axes and add a title for clarity. For example:

R

```
ggplot(data, aes(x = variable1, y = variable2)) +
  geom_point() +
  labs(title = "Scatter Plot of Variable1 vs Variable2", x =
"Variable1", y = "Variable2")
```

2. Enhancing Plots with Themes and Labels: Take your plots to the next level by customizing the appearance with themes and adding informative labels. Experiment with different `theme()` options in `ggplot2` to find a style that suits your data. Additionally, use `geom_text()` to add annotations directly to your plots. For instance:

R

```
ggplot(data, aes(x = variable1, y = variable2)) +
  geom_point() +
  theme_minimal() +
  labs(title = "Enhanced Scatter Plot", x = "Variable1", y =
"Variable2") +
  geom_text(aes(label = names), vjust = -1)
```

3. Interactive Plots with plotly: Convert a `ggplot2` plot into an interactive `plotly` plot to allow users to explore the data more deeply. Use the `ggplotly()` function to transform your static plot into an interactive visualization. For example:

R

```
library(plotly)
p <- ggplot(data, aes(x = variable1, y = variable2)) +
  geom_point()
ggplotly(p)
```

4. Dynamic Visualization with plotly: Create a dynamic plot that lets users interact with the visualization, such as zooming in/out or hovering over points to display additional information. Utilize `plot_ly()` to build these interactive components from scratch. For instance:

R

```
plot_ly(data, x = ~variable1, y = ~variable2, type = 'scatter',
mode = 'markers',
        marker = list(size = 10), hoverinfo = 'text', text =
~paste('Value:', variable3))
```

These visualization exercises are designed to refine your ability to craft narratives around your data, making it easier for your audience to understand and engage with your findings. As you progress, remember to explore the vast array of functionalities both `ggplot2` and `plotly` offer, pushing the boundaries of your data visualization capabilities.

Data Import and Cleaning Exercises

Description

Import the CSV file `employee_data.csv` into R without converting strings to factors. Then, identify and remove any rows that contain missing values.

R
```
# Your code here
```

Expected output

A cleaned data frame named `clean_employee_data` with all rows containing missing values removed.

Solution

R
```
employee_data <- read.csv("employee_data.csv", stringsAsFactors = FALSE)
clean_employee_data <- na.omit(employee_data)
```

Efficient solution explanation

Using `read.csv()` with `stringsAsFactors = FALSE` ensures that string columns remain as character vectors, simplifying data manipulation. The `na.omit()` function efficiently removes any rows with missing values, resulting in a clean dataset ready for analysis.

Data Visualization Exercises

5. **Faceted Plots with ggplot2**: Create faceted plots to display multiple plots based on a categorical variable, allowing for easy comparison across different groups. Use the `facet_wrap()` or `facet_grid()` functions to achieve this. For example, visualize the

relationship between `variable1` and `variable2` across different categories in `variable3`:

R

```
ggplot(data, aes(x = variable1, y = variable2)) +
  geom_point() +
  facet_wrap(~ variable3) +
  labs(title = "Faceted Scatter Plots by Variable3", x =
"Variable1", y = "Variable2")
```

6. **Heatmaps and Correlation Plots**: Generate heatmaps to visualize the correlation between multiple variables in your dataset. Use the `geom_tile()` function in `ggplot2` combined with a correlation matrix. For example:

R

```
library(reshape2)
correlation_matrix <- cor(data[ , sapply(data, is.numeric)])
melted_corr <- melt(correlation_matrix)
ggplot(melted_corr, aes(x = Var1, y = Var2, fill = value)) +
  geom_tile() +
  scale_fill_gradient2(low = "blue", high = "red", mid =
"white",
                       midpoint = 0, limit = c(-1,1), space =
"Lab",
                       name="Correlation") +
  theme_minimal() +
  labs(title = "Correlation Heatmap", x = "", y = "")
```

7. **Time Series Visualization**: Plot time series data to analyze trends over time. Use `geom_line()` to create line charts and handle date or datetime data appropriately. For example, visualize sales over time:

R

```
ggplot(data, aes(x = date, y = sales)) +
  geom_line(color = "steelblue") +
```

```
    labs(title = "Sales Over Time", x = "Date", y = "Sales") +
    theme_minimal()
```

8. **Geospatial Data Visualization**: Visualize geographical data using `ggplot2` along with the `sf` package for handling spatial data. Create maps to display data points or regions. For example, map the distribution of a variable across different states:

R
```
    library(sf)
    library(ggplot2)
    # Assume 'states_sf' is an sf object with state geometries and
a 'value' column
    ggplot(states_sf) +
      geom_sf(aes(fill = value)) +
      scale_fill_viridis_c() +
      labs(title = "Geographical Distribution of Value by State",
fill = "Value") +
      theme_minimal()
```

9. **Customizing Legends and Scales**: Enhance your plots by customizing legends and scales to improve readability and aesthetics. Modify elements such as legend position, title, and the scales of axes. For example, adjust the legend position and customize color scales:

R
```
    ggplot(data, aes(x = variable1, y = variable2, color =
category)) +
      geom_point() +
      scale_color_manual(values = c("Category1" = "purple",
"Category2" = "orange")) +
      theme_minimal() +
      labs(title = "Customized Legends and Color Scales", x =
"Variable1", y = "Variable2") +
      theme(legend.position = "bottom", legend.title =
element_text(size = 12))
```

10. **Saving and Exporting Plots**: Learn to save your visualizations in various formats for presentations, reports, or further analysis. Use the `ggsave()` function to export your plots. Specify the filename, format, and dimensions as needed. For example:

R

```
plot <- ggplot(data, aes(x = variable1, y = variable2)) +
    geom_point() +
    labs(title = "Scatter Plot to Save", x = "Variable1", y =
"Variable2")
    ggsave(filename = "scatter_plot.png", plot = plot, width = 8,
height = 6, dpi = 300)
```

These additional exercises will deepen your understanding of data visualization in R, allowing you to create more complex and informative graphics. Experiment with different functions and customization options to discover the full potential of `ggplot2` and `plotly` in presenting your data effectively.

Data Analysis and Statistical Modeling Exercises

Description

Load the `housing_data.csv` file into R and create a scatter plot to visualize the relationship between `SquareFeet` and `Price`. Ensure that the plot includes appropriate axis labels and a title.

R

```
# Your code here
```

Expected output

A scatter plot displaying `SquareFeet` on the x-axis and `Price` on the y-axis, with labeled axes and an appropriate title.

Solution

R

```
# Import the data
housing_data <- read.csv("housing_data.csv", stringsAsFactors =
FALSE)
```

```
# Create the scatter plot
plot(housing_data$SquareFeet, housing_data$Price,
     xlab = "Square Feet",
     ylab = "Price (USD)",
     main = "Relationship Between Square Feet and Price")
```

Efficient solution explanation

Using `read.csv()` with `stringsAsFactors = FALSE` ensures that string data remains as character vectors, which is useful for data manipulation. The `plot()` function creates a scatter plot with `SquareFeet` and `Price`, while the `xlab`, `ylab`, and `main` parameters add clear axis labels and a descriptive title, enhancing the visualization's readability.

Programming Challenges

Programming Challenges

1. **Automate Data Import and Cleaning Pipeline**: Create a script that imports multiple CSV files from a directory, combines them into a single data frame, and performs data cleaning operations such as handling missing values and converting data types. Use functions like **list**.files(), lapply(), and dplyr functions to streamline the process.

R

```
# List all CSV files in the directory
file_list <- list.files(path = "data/", pattern = "*.csv",
full.names = TRUE)
# Import and combine all CSV files
combined_data <- do.call(rbind, lapply(file_list, read.csv))
# Handle missing values by replacing with median
combined_data$column[is.na(combined_data$column)] <-
median(combined_data$column, na.rm = TRUE)
# Convert column to factor
combined_data$category <- as.factor(combined_data$category)
```

2. **Build a Custom Function for Summary Statistics**: Write a function named `custom_summary` that takes a data frame and a numeric column name as inputs and returns the mean, median, standard deviation, and count of non-missing values for that column.

R

```r
custom_summary <- function(data, column) {
  mean_val <- mean(data[[column]], na.rm = TRUE)
  median_val <- median(data[[column]], na.rm = TRUE)
  sd_val <- sd(data[[column]], na.rm = TRUE)
  count <- sum(!is.na(data[[column]]))
  return(list(Mean = mean_val, Median = median_val,
              Standard_Deviation = sd_val, Count = count))
}
# Example usage
summary_stats <- custom_summary(combined_data, "sales")
print(summary_stats)
```

3. **Create an Interactive Dashboard with Shiny**: Develop a simple Shiny app that allows users to upload a dataset, select variables for visualization, and generate interactive plots using `ggplot2` and `plotly`. Incorporate input controls such as dropdown menus and sliders to enhance user interaction.

R

```r
library(shiny)
library(ggplot2)
library(plotly)
ui <- fluidPage(
  titlePanel("Interactive Data Visualization"),
  sidebarLayout(
    sidebarPanel(
      fileInput("file", "Upload CSV File"),
      uiOutput("varselect")
```

```r
      ),
      mainPanel(
        plotlyOutput("plot")
      )
    )
  )

  server <- function(input, output, session) {
    data <- reactive({
      req(input$file)
      read.csv(input$file$datapath)
    })
    output$varselect <- renderUI({
      df <- data()
      if(is.null(df)) return(NULL)
      tagList(
        selectInput("xvar", "X-axis Variable", choices =
names(df)),
        selectInput("yvar", "Y-axis Variable", choices =
names(df))
      )
    })
    output$plot <- renderPlotly({
      req(input$xvar, input$yvar)
      p <- ggplot(data(), aes_string(x = input$xvar, y =
input$yvar)) +
        geom_point() +
        theme_minimal()
      ggplotly(p)
    })
  }
  shinyApp(ui, server)
```

4. **Develop a Data Transformation Pipeline Using dplyr**: Utilize the `dplyr` package to perform a series of data transformations, including filtering rows, selecting specific columns, creating new calculated columns, and summarizing data grouped by a categorical variable.

R

```r
library(dplyr)
transformed_data <- combined_data %>%
    filter(!is.na(sales) & sales > 0) %>%
    select(date, category, sales, region) %>%
    mutate(sales_per_day = sales / as.numeric(as.Date(date))) %>%
    group_by(category) %>%
    summarize(total_sales = sum(sales), average_sales =
mean(sales))
  print(transformed_data)
```

5. **Implement a Linear Regression Model**: Fit a linear regression model to predict a numeric outcome variable based on one or more predictor variables. Evaluate the model by checking assumptions, interpreting coefficients, and visualizing residuals.

R

```r
# Fit the model
model <- lm(sales ~ advertising + price, data = combined_data)
# Summary of the model
summary(model)
# Plot residuals
plot(model$residuals)
abline(h = 0, col = "red")
```

6. **Perform Text Analysis on a Dataset**: Use text mining techniques to analyze text data within your dataset. Clean the text by removing stop words and punctuation, create a term-document matrix, and visualize the most frequent terms using a word cloud.

R

```r
library(tm)
```

```
library(wordcloud)
# Create a corpus
corpus <- Corpus(VectorSource(combined_data$text_column))
# Text cleaning
corpus <- tm_map(corpus, content_transformer(tolower))
corpus <- tm_map(corpus, removePunctuation)
corpus <- tm_map(corpus, removeWords, stopwords("english"))
# Create term-document matrix
tdm <- TermDocumentMatrix(corpus)
matrix <- as.matrix(tdm)
word_freq <- sort(rowSums(matrix), decreasing = TRUE)
df <- data.frame(word = names(word_freq), freq = word_freq)
# Generate word cloud
wordcloud(words = df$word, freq = df$freq, min.freq = 2, colors
= brewer.pal(8, "Dark2"))
```

7. **Optimize Code with Vectorization**: Refactor a loop-based computation to use vectorized operations for improved performance. Compare the execution time of both implementations using the `system.time()` function.

R

```
# Loop-based implementation
loop_result <- numeric(length(combined_data$sales))
system.time({
  for(i in 1:length(combined_data$sales)) {
    loop_result[i] <- combined_data$sales[i] * 2
  }
})
# Vectorized implementation
system.time({
  vector_result <- combined_data$sales * 2
})
# Verify results are identical
all(loop_result == vector_result)
```

8. Create a Function for Batch Plot Generation: Write a function that takes a dataset and a list of variable pairs, then generates and saves scatter plots for each pair automatically. Incorporate error handling to manage cases where variables may not exist or are not numeric.

R

```r
generate_scatter_plots <- function(data, var_pairs, output_dir
= "plots/") {
    if(!dir.exists(output_dir)) {
      dir.create(output_dir)
    }
    for(pair in var_pairs) {
      x <- pair[1]
      y <- pair[2]
      if(!(x %in% names(data)) | !(y %in% names(data))) {
        warning(paste("Variables", x, "and/or", y, "not found in
data. Skipping."))
        next
      }
      if(!is.numeric(data[[x]]) | !is.numeric(data[[y]])) {
        warning(paste("Variables", x, "and/or", y, "are not
numeric. Skipping."))
        next
      }
      p <- ggplot(data, aes_string(x = x, y = y)) +
        geom_point() +
        theme_minimal() +
        labs(title = paste("Scatter Plot of", x, "vs", y))
        ggsave(filename = paste0(output_dir, "scatter_", x, "_vs_",
y, ".png"), plot = p)
    }
}
# Example usage
```

```r
    variable_pairs <- list(c("advertising", "sales"), c("price",
"sales"), c("invalid_var", "sales"))

    generate_scatter_plots(combined_data, variable_pairs)
```

9. **Build and Document an R Package**: Develop a simple R package that includes custom functions you've created throughout the book. Use `roxygen2` for documentation, write unit tests with `testthat`, and ensure the package structure follows best practices. Finally, install and load your package to verify its functionality.

R

```r
    library(devtools)
    library(roxygen2)
    library(testthat)
    # Create package structure
    create_package("myDataTools")
    # Navigate to package directory
    setwd("myDataTools")
    # Add a function
    usethis::use_r("custom_summary")
    writeLines('
    # Custom Summary Function
    #
    # Calculates mean, median, standard deviation, and count for a
numeric column.
    #
    # @param data A data frame.
    # @param column The numeric column to summarize.
    # @return A list with summary statistics.
    # @export
    custom_summary <- function(data, column) {
      mean_val <- mean(data[[column]], na.rm = TRUE)
      median_val <- median(data[[column]], na.rm = TRUE)
      sd_val <- sd(data[[column]], na.rm = TRUE)
```

```r
    count <- sum(!is.na(data[[column]]))
    return(list(Mean = mean_val, Median = median_val,
              Standard_Deviation = sd_val, Count = count))
}
', con = "R/custom_summary.R")
# Document the package
document()
# Add tests
usethis::use_test("custom_summary")
writeLines('
test_that("custom_summary works correctly", {
    df <- data.frame(values = c(1, 2, 3, 4, 5, NA))
    result <- custom_summary(df, "values")
    expect_equal(result$Mean, 3)
    expect_equal(result$Median, 3)
    expect_equal(result$Standard_Deviation, sd(c(1,2,3,4,5)))
    expect_equal(result$Count, 5)
})
', con = "tests/testthat/test-custom_summary.R")
# Run tests
test()
# Install the package
install()
# Load the package
library(myDataTools)
# Use the function from the package
summary_stats <- custom_summary(combined_data, "sales")
print(summary_stats)
```

10. **Develop a Time Series Forecasting Script**: Create a script that imports time series data, decomposes it into trend, seasonality, and residuals, fits a forecasting model using `forecast` package, and visualizes the forecasted values along with confidence intervals.

```R
library(forecast)
library(ggplot2)
# Import time series data
ts_data <- ts(combined_data$sales, start = c(2020, 1),
frequency = 12)
# Decompose the time series
decomposed <- decompose(ts_data)
plot(decomposed)
# Fit an ARIMA model
fit <- auto.arima(ts_data)
summary(fit)
# Forecast the next 12 periods
forecasted <- forecast(fit, h = 12)
plot(forecasted)
# Convert forecast to data frame for ggplot
forecast_df <- data.frame(
  Time = time(forecasted),
  Forecast = as.numeric(forecasted$mean),
  Lower = as.numeric(forecasted$lower[,2]),
  Upper = as.numeric(forecasted$upper[,2])
)
# Plot with ggplot2
ggplot() +
  geom_line(aes(x = time(ts_data), y = ts_data), color =
"blue") +
  geom_line(aes(x = forecast_df$Time, y =
forecast_df$Forecast), color = "red") +
  geom_ribbon(aes(x = forecast_df$Time, ymin =
forecast_df$Lower, ymax = forecast_df$Upper),
              alpha = 0.2, fill = "orange") +
  labs(title = "Sales Forecast", x = "Time", y = "Sales") +
  theme_minimal()
```

11. Implement a Supervised Machine Learning Model: Use the `caret` package to train a classification model on a dataset. Perform data splitting, model training with cross-validation, evaluate model performance using confusion matrix and ROC curve, and identify important features.

R

```r
library(caret)
library(pROC)
# Prepare data
set.seed(123)
trainIndex <- createDataPartition(combined_data$target, p = 0.7,
                                  list = FALSE,
                                  times = 1)
trainData <- combined_data[trainIndex, ]
testData <- combined_data[-trainIndex, ]
# Train a logistic regression model with cross-validation
control <- trainControl(method = "cv", number = 5, classProbs = TRUE,
                        summaryFunction = twoClassSummary)
model <- train(target ~ ., data = trainData, method = "glm",
               family = "binomial", trControl = control, metric = "ROC")
# Predict on test data
predictions <- predict(model, testData)
prob_predictions <- predict(model, testData, type = "prob")
# Evaluate performance
confusionMatrix(predictions, testData$target)
# ROC Curve
roc_obj <- roc(testData$target, prob_predictions$Yes)
plot(roc_obj, main = "ROC Curve")
# Feature Importance
importance <- varImp(model, scale = FALSE)
```

```r
    print(importance)

    plot(importance, main = "Feature Importance")
```

12. **Create a Shiny Application for Interactive Data Exploration**: Develop a Shiny app that allows users to interactively filter data based on multiple criteria, select variables for analysis, and dynamically update visualizations based on user input.

R

```r
    library(shiny)

    library(ggplot2)

    library(dplyr)

    ui <- fluidPage(

       titlePanel("Interactive Data Explorer"),

       sidebarLayout(

          sidebarPanel(

             selectInput("category", "Select Category", choices =
unique(combined_data$category), selected =
unique(combined_data$category), multiple = TRUE),

             sliderInput("salesRange", "Sales Range", min =
min(combined_data$sales, na.rm = TRUE),

                         max = max(combined_data$sales, na.rm = TRUE),
value = c(min(combined_data$sales, na.rm = TRUE),
max(combined_data$sales, na.rm = TRUE)))

          ),

          mainPanel(

             plotOutput("scatterPlot")

          )

       )

    )

    server <- function(input, output) {

       filtered_data <- reactive({

          combined_data %>%

             filter(category %in% input$category,

                    sales >= input$salesRange[1],
```

```
                    sales <= input$salesRange[2])
    })
    output$scatterPlot <- renderPlot({
        ggplot(filtered_data(), aes(x = advertising, y = sales,
color = category)) +
            geom_point() +
            theme_minimal() +
            labs(title = "Advertising vs Sales", x = "Advertising
Budget", y = "Sales")
    })
    }
    shinyApp(ui, server)
```

13. **Optimize Data Processing with Parallel Computing**: Implement parallel processing to speed up data-intensive tasks. Use the `parallel` package to execute operations across multiple CPU cores, such as applying a function to large datasets.

R
```
library(parallel)
# Detect number of cores
num_cores <- detectCores() - 1
# Initialize cluster
cl <- makeCluster(num_cores)
# Export necessary variables/functions to cluster
clusterExport(cl, varlist = c("combined_data"))
# Define a function to apply
compute_square <- function(x) {
    return(x^2)
}
# Apply function in parallel
sales_squared <- parSapply(cl, combined_data$sales,
compute_square)
# Stop cluster
```

```r
    stopCluster(cl)
    # Add results to data frame
    combined_data$sales_squared <- sales_squared
```

14. **Develop a Custom Data Validation Function**: Create a function that checks for data integrity by validating that certain columns meet specified criteria, such as ranges for numerical values or formats for categorical variables. The function should return a report of any discrepancies found.

R

```r
    validate_data <- function(data) {
      report <- list()
      # Check for sales being non-negative
      negative_sales <- sum(data$sales < 0, na.rm = TRUE)
      if(negative_sales > 0) {
        report$negative_sales <- negative_sales
      }
      # Check if dates are in correct format
      if(!all(!is.na(as.Date(data$date, format = "%Y-%m-%d")))) {
        report$invalid_dates <- sum(is.na(as.Date(data$date, format
= "%Y-%m-%d")))
      }
      # Check if category is within expected levels
      expected_categories <- c("A", "B", "C")
      invalid_categories <- sum(!data$category %in%
expected_categories, na.rm = TRUE)
      if(invalid_categories > 0) {
        report$invalid_categories <- invalid_categories
      }
      return(report)
    }
    # Example usage
    validation_report <- validate_data(combined_data)
```

```
print(validation_report)
```

15. **Integrate External APIs for Data Retrieval**: Write a script that connects to an external API to fetch real-time data, processes the JSON response, and integrates it with your existing dataset. Handle authentication and potential errors gracefully.

R

```
library(httr)
library(jsonlite)
library(dplyr)
# Define API endpoint and parameters
api_url <- "https://api.example.com/data"
api_key <- "your_api_key_here"
# Make GET request
response <- GET(api_url, add_headers(Authorization =
paste("Bearer", api_key)))
# Check for successful response
if(status_code(response) == 200) {
  data_json <- content(response, "text")
  data_parsed <- fromJSON(data_json, flatten = TRUE)
  # Convert to data frame
  api_data <- as.data.frame(data_parsed)
  # Integrate with existing data
  combined_dataset <- left_join(combined_data, api_data, by =
"common_column")
  } else {
  stop("API request failed with status: ",
status_code(response))
```

16. **Implement a Cross-Validation Workflow for Model Selection**: Develop a systematic approach to evaluate multiple machine learning models using cross-validation. Compare models based on performance metrics and select the best-performing one for your dataset.

```R
library(caret)
# Define training control with 10-fold cross-validation
train_control <- trainControl(method = "cv", number = 10,
classProbs = TRUE, summaryFunction = twoClassSummary)
# Define models to compare
models <- c("glm", "rf", "svmRadial")
# Initialize results container
results <- list()
# Iterate over models
for(model in models) {
  set.seed(123)
  fit <- train(target ~ ., data = combined_data, method = model,
                 trControl = train_control, metric = "ROC")
  results[[model]] <- fit
}
# Compare results
res <- resamples(results)
summary(res)
dotplot(res)
```

17. Create a Script for Automated Reporting with R Markdown: Develop an R script that generates a comprehensive report automatically by rendering an R Markdown document. Include sections for data summary, visualizations, and model results, ensuring the report updates with new data inputs.

```R
library(rmarkdown)
# Define parameters
params <- list(data_path = "data/combined_data.csv")
# Render the R Markdown document
render(input = "report_template.Rmd",
```

```r
    output_file = "Automated_Report.html",
    params = params,
    envir = new.env())
```

18. **Build a Real-Time Data Monitoring Tool**: Use R to create a monitoring tool that tracks specific metrics in real-time, updates visualizations dynamically, and sends alerts if certain thresholds are exceeded. Incorporate packages like `shiny` and `shinydashboard` for the user interface.

R

```r
    library(shiny)
    library(shinydashboard)
    library(plotly)
    ui <- dashboardPage(
      dashboardHeader(title = "Real-Time Monitoring"),
      dashboardSidebar(
        sidebarMenu(
          menuItem("Dashboard", tabName = "dashboard", icon =
icon("dashboard"))
        )
      ),
      dashboardBody(
        tabItems(
          tabItem(tabName = "dashboard",
                  fluidRow(
                    box(title = "Metric 1", status = "primary",
solidHeader = TRUE,
                        plotlyOutput("metric1Plot")),
                    box(title = "Metric 2", status = "warning",
solidHeader = TRUE,
                        plotlyOutput("metric2Plot"))
                  )
          )
```

```r
            )
        )
    )

    server <- function(input, output, session) {
      # Simulate real-time data
      metric1 <- reactiveVal(0)
      metric2 <- reactiveVal(0)
      observe({
          invalidateLater(1000, session)
          metric1(metric1() + rnorm(1))
          metric2(metric2() + rnorm(1))
          # Send alert if thresholds are exceeded
          if(metric1() > 5) {
              showNotification("Metric 1 has exceeded the threshold!",
type = "error")
          }
          if(metric2() < -5) {
              showNotification("Metric 2 has dropped below the
threshold!", type = "warning")
          }
      })
      output$metric1Plot <- renderPlotly({
          plot_ly(x = Sys.time(), y = metric1(), type = 'scatter',
mode = 'lines+markers') %>%
              layout(title = "Metric 1 Over Time", xaxis = list(title =
"Time"), yaxis = list(title = "Value"))
      })
      output$metric2Plot <- renderPlotly({
          plot_ly(x = Sys.time(), y = metric2(), type = 'scatter',
mode = 'lines+markers') %>%
              layout(title = "Metric 2 Over Time", xaxis = list(title =
"Time"), yaxis = list(title = "Value"))
      })
```

```
}
shinyApp(ui, server)
```

18. **Optimize Database Queries with DBI and dplyr**: Connect to a SQL database using the DBI package and perform data manipulation operations using dplyr. Optimize your queries to handle large datasets efficiently by selecting only necessary columns and filtering data at the database level.

R

```
library(DBI)
library(dplyr)
# Establish database connection
con <- dbConnect(RSQLite::SQLite(), dbname = "example.db")
# Reference a table
db_table <- tbl(con, "sales_data")
# Perform data manipulation with dplyr
filtered_data <- db_table %>%
  filter(category == "A", sales > 1000) %>%
  select(date, sales, region) %>%
  arrange(desc(sales)) %>%
  collect()
# Disconnect from the database
dbDisconnect(con)
print(filtered_data)
```

19. **Implement Regular Expressions for Advanced Text Processing**: Use regular expressions to extract specific patterns from text data. For example, extract email addresses from a text column or validate the format of certain entries.

R

```
library(stringr)
# Extract email addresses
combined_data$emails <- str_extract(combined_data$text_column,
"[a-zA-Z0-9._%+-]+@[a-zA-Z0-9.-]+\\.[a-z]{2,}")
```

```r
    # Validate phone numbers (e.g., format: (123) 456-7890)
    combined_data$valid_phone <-
str_detect(combined_data$phone_number, "^\<img src="https://
plottybot.com/img/math//5a/78/
a9/5a78a9579de710196f8619b8e27f58c0.png" alt="Formula"
style="vertical-align:middle;" /> \\d{3}-\\d{4}$")
    # Remove rows with invalid phone numbers
    cleaned_data <- combined_data %>% filter(valid_phone == TRUE)
```

20. **Create an Automated Data Backup Script**: Develop a script that automatically backs up your important datasets at regular intervals. Incorporate error handling to ensure backups are successful and log the status of each backup operation.

R

```r
    library(file.copy)
    backup_data <- function(source_dir, backup_dir) {
      # Get current date
      date_stamp <- format(Sys.Date(), "%Y%m%d")
      # Create backup directory if it doesn't exist
      if(!dir.exists(backup_dir)) {
        dir.create(backup_dir)
      }
      # Define backup file name
      backup_file <- paste0("backup_", date_stamp, ".csv")
      # Attempt to copy the file
      tryCatch({
        file.copy(from = file.path(source_dir,
"combined_data.csv"),
                  to = file.path(backup_dir, backup_file))
        message("Backup successful: ", backup_file)
      }, error = function(e) {
        message("Backup failed: ", e)
      })
    }
```

```
# Example usage
backup_data(source_dir = "data/", backup_dir = "backups/")
```

These programming challenges are designed to test and enhance your R skills across various domains, including data manipulation, visualization, modeling, and application development. Tackle these exercises to build a robust understanding of R and its capabilities in data analysis and beyond.</h3>

Text Data Handling Exercises

<h3>Text Data Handling Exercises

1. **Extract Specific Patterns Using Regular Expressions**: Utilize regular expressions to identify and extract email addresses from a text column in your dataset. This exercise will help you practice pattern matching and data extraction techniques.

R
```
library(stringr)
# Sample data
data <- data.frame(text = c("Contact us at
support@example.com",
                            "Send an email to info@domain.org
for more info",
                            "No email here"))
# Extract email addresses
data$emails <- str_extract(data$text, "[a-zA-Z0-9._%+-]+@[a-zA-Z0-9.-]+\\.[a-z]{2,}")
print(data)
```

2. **Clean and Standardize Text Data**: Practice cleaning text data by converting all text to lowercase, removing punctuation, and eliminating stop words. This is essential for preparing text data for analysis.

R
```
library(tm)
```

```r
# Sample text data
data <- data.frame(text = c("Hello World!", "Data Analysis with
R.", "Cleaning TEXT data is fun."))
# Create a corpus
corpus <- Corpus(VectorSource(data$text))
# Text cleaning steps
corpus <- tm_map(corpus, content_transformer(tolower))
corpus <- tm_map(corpus, removePunctuation)
corpus <- tm_map(corpus, removeWords, stopwords("english"))
# Convert back to data frame
cleaned_text <- sapply(corpus, as.character)
data$cleaned_text <- cleaned_text
print(data)
```

3. **Tokenize Text Data into Words**: Break down sentences into individual words using tokenization. This exercise will help you understand how to work with word-level data for further analysis.

R

```r
library(tidytext)
library(dplyr)
# Sample data
data <- data.frame(id = 1:2, text = c("Data science is
fascinating.",

                                "R is a powerful tool for
data analysis."))
# Tokenize into words
tokens <- data %>%
   unnest_tokens(word, text)
print(tokens)
```

4. Perform Sentiment Analysis on Text Data: Analyze the sentiment of text entries using the `tidytext` package. This exercise introduces you to sentiment scoring and interpretation.

R

```r
library(tidytext)
library(dplyr)
# Sample data
data <- data.frame(id = 1:3, text = c("I love sunny days",
                                        "This is a terrible mistake",
                                        "Feeling happy and joyful"))
# Tokenize and join with sentiment lexicon
sentiments <- data %>%
  unnest_tokens(word, text) %>%
  inner_join(get_sentiments("bing")) %>%
  count(id, sentiment) %>%
  spread(sentiment, n, fill = 0) %>%
  mutate(sentiment_score = positive - negative)
print(sentiments)
```

5. Create a Term-Document Matrix: Build a term-document matrix to visualize the frequency of words across different documents. This is a foundational step for various text mining techniques.

R

```r
library(tm)
# Sample data
data <- data.frame(doc_id = 1:3, text = c("R is great for data analysis.",
                                           "Data visualization is key.",
                                           "Machine learning with R is powerful."))
# Create a corpus
```

```
corpus <- Corpus(VectorSource(data$text))
# Create term-document matrix
tdm <- TermDocumentMatrix(corpus)
print(tdm)
```

6. Generate a Word Cloud from Text Data

6. **Generate a Word Cloud from Text Data**: Visualize the most frequent words in your text data using a word cloud. This exercise helps in identifying prominent terms at a glance.

R

```
library(wordcloud)
library(tm)
# Sample data
data <- data.frame(text = c("Data science with R is versatile.",
                    "Visualization brings data to life.",
                    "Machine learning enhances data analysis."))
# Create a corpus
corpus <- Corpus(VectorSource(data$text))
corpus <- tm_map(corpus, content_transformer(tolower))
corpus <- tm_map(corpus, removePunctuation)
corpus <- tm_map(corpus, removeWords, stopwords("english"))
# Create term-document matrix and calculate word frequencies
tdm <- TermDocumentMatrix(corpus)
matrix <- as.matrix(tdm)
word_freq <- sort(rowSums(matrix), decreasing = TRUE)
df <- data.frame(word = names(word_freq), freq = word_freq)
# Generate word cloud
wordcloud(words = df$word, freq = df$freq, min.freq = 1, colors = brewer.pal(8, "Dark2"))
```

7. **Implement N-gram Analysis**: Analyze sequences of words (n-grams) to understand common phrases and patterns in your text data. This is useful for more nuanced text analysis.

```R
library(tidytext)
library(dplyr)
# Sample data
data <- data.frame(id = 1:2, text = c("R is excellent for data analysis.",
                                        "Data visualization with R is intuitive."))
# Create bigrams
bigrams <- data %>%
  unnest_tokens(bigram, text, token = "ngrams", n = 2)
print(bigrams)
```

8. **Identify Most Frequent Words After Cleaning**: After cleaning your text data, identify the most frequently occurring words to understand key themes and topics.

```R
library(tidytext)
library(dplyr)
# Sample data
data <- data.frame(id = 1:3, text = c("R is great for data analysis.",
                                        "Visualization with R enhances understanding.",
                                        "Data analysis and visualization go hand in hand."))
# Tokenize and clean
tokens <- data %>%
  unnest_tokens(word, text) %>%
  anti_join(get_stopwords())
# Count word frequencies
word_freq <- tokens %>%
  count(word, sort = TRUE)
print(word_freq)
```

9. Detect and Remove Duplicate Entries in Text Data: Ensure data integrity by identifying and removing duplicate text entries from your dataset.

R

```
library(dplyr)
# Sample data with duplicates
data <- data.frame(id = 1:5, text = c("Data analysis in R.",
                                       "Data visualization is
powerful.",
                                       "Data analysis in R.",
                                       "Machine learning with R.",
                                       "Data visualization is
powerful."))
# Remove duplicates
unique_data <- data %>%
  distinct(text, .keep_all = TRUE)
print(unique_data)
```

10. Extract and Validate URLs from Text Data: Identify and extract URLs from text entries, ensuring they follow a valid format. This is useful for analyzing web references within your data.

R

```
library(stringr)
library(dplyr)
# Sample data
data <- data.frame(id = 1:3, text = c("Visit our website at
https://www.example.com for more info.",
                      "Check out http://invalid-url for details.",
                      "No URL here."))
# Extract URLs
data$urls <- str_extract(data$text, "(http|https)://[^\\s]+")
# Validate URLs (basic validation)
data$valid_url <- str_detect(data$urls, "^https?://[A-Za-
z0-9.-]+\\.[A-Za-z]{2,}(/\\S*)?$")
print(data)
```

These exercises provide hands-on experience with handling and analyzing text data in R. By working through them, you'll enhance your ability to preprocess, manipulate, and extract meaningful insights from textual information.</h3>

Time Series Analysis Exercises

Description

Load the `weather_data.csv` file, which contains daily temperature readings for the past year. Convert the `Date` column to a Date object and create a time series object for the `Temperature` data. Plot the time series and add a 7-day moving average to smooth the temperature trends.

```R
# Your code here
```

Expected output

A time series plot of daily temperatures with a 7-day moving average line overlayed, illustrating the temperature trends over the year.

Solution

```R
# Import the data
weather_data <- read.csv("weather_data.csv", stringsAsFactors = FALSE)
# Convert Date column to Date type
weather_data$Date <- as.Date(weather_data$Date, format = "%Y-%m-%d")
# Create time series object
temperature_ts <- ts(weather_data$Temperature, start = c(2023, 1), frequency = 365)
# Plot the time series
plot(temperature_ts, main = "Daily Temperatures Over One Year", xlab = "Day", ylab = "Temperature (°F)")
# Add 7-day moving average
```

```
ma7 <- stats::filter(temperature_ts, rep(1/7, 7), sides = 2)
lines(ma7, col = "red")
```

Efficient solution explanation

Using `read.csv()` with `stringsAsFactors = FALSE` ensures that the `Date` column remains as character vectors for easy conversion. The `as.Date()` function transforms the `Date` column into Date objects, which are essential for creating an accurate time series. The `ts()` function constructs a time series object with a specified start time and frequency (365 for daily data). The `plot()` function visualizes the daily temperature data, while the `stats::filter()` function computes a 7-day moving average to smooth out short-term fluctuations. The `lines()` function then overlays the moving average on the plot in red, highlighting the overall temperature trend.

Machine Learning Exercises

Machine Learning Exercises

1. **Build a Logistic Regression Model**: Utilize logistic regression to predict a binary outcome. Split your dataset into training and testing sets, train the model, and evaluate its performance using a confusion matrix.

R

```
library(caret)
# Load dataset
data(iris)
# Convert Species to binary outcome
iris$Species <- ifelse(iris$Species == "setosa", "Yes", "No")
# Split data into training and testing sets
set.seed(123)
trainIndex <- createDataPartition(iris$Species, p = 0.7, list = FALSE)
trainData <- iris[trainIndex, ]
testData  <- iris[-trainIndex, ]
# Train logistic regression model
```

```r
model <- glm(Species ~ Sepal.Length + Sepal.Width +
Petal.Length + Petal.Width,
                    data = trainData, family = binomial)
# Predict probabilities
probabilities <- predict(model, testData, type = "response")
# Convert probabilities to class labels
predictions <- ifelse(probabilities > 0.5, "Yes", "No")
# Evaluate model performance
confusionMatrix(as.factor(predictions),
as.factor(testData$Species))
```

2. **Perform k-Nearest Neighbors Classification**: Implement the k-NN algorithm to classify data points based on their nearest neighbors. Experiment with different values of *k* to determine the optimal number of neighbors.

R

```r
library(caret)
# Load dataset
data(iris)
# Split data into training and testing sets
set.seed(123)
trainIndex <- createDataPartition(iris$Species, p = 0.7, list =
FALSE)
trainData <- iris[trainIndex, ]
testData  <- iris[-trainIndex, ]
# Train k-NN model with k = 3
model <- train(Species ~ ., data = trainData, method = "knn",
          trControl = trainControl(method = "cv", number = 5),
          tuneGrid = data.frame(k = 3))
# Predict on test data
predictions <- predict(model, testData)
# Evaluate model performance
confusionMatrix(predictions, testData$Species)
```

3. **Implement Decision Tree Classification**: Use decision trees to model the relationship between features and target variables. Visualize the tree structure and interpret the decision paths.

R

```
library(rpart)
library(rpart.plot)
# Load dataset
data(iris)
# Train decision tree model
tree_model <- rpart(Species ~ ., data = iris, method = "class")
# Plot the decision tree
rpart.plot(tree_model, type = 3, extra = 102, fallen.leaves = TRUE)
```

4. **Conduct Principal Component Analysis (PCA)**: Perform PCA to reduce the dimensionality of your dataset. Visualize the principal components and interpret the variance explained by each component.

R

```
library(ggplot2)
# Load dataset
data(iris)
# Perform PCA
pca_result <- prcomp(iris[, -5], center = TRUE, scale. = TRUE)
# Summary of PCA
summary(pca_result)
# Create a data frame with principal components
pca_data <- data.frame(pca_result$x, Species = iris$Species)
# Plot the first two principal components
ggplot(pca_data, aes(x = PC1, y = PC2, color = Species)) +
   geom_point(size = 2) +
```

```
      labs(title = "PCA of Iris Dataset", x = "Principal Component
1", y = "Principal Component 2") +
      theme_minimal()
```

5. **Build a Support Vector Machine (SVM) Model**: Train an SVM classifier to separate different classes in your dataset. Experiment with different kernels and assess the model's accuracy.

R

```
    library(e1071)
    library(caret)
    # Load dataset
    data(iris)
    # Split data into training and testing sets
    set.seed(123)
    trainIndex <- createDataPartition(iris$Species, p = 0.7, list =
FALSE)
    trainData <- iris[trainIndex, ]
    testData  <- iris[-trainIndex, ]
    # Train SVM model with radial kernel
    svm_model <- svm(Species ~ ., data = trainData, kernel =
"radial", probability = TRUE)
    # Predict on test data
    predictions <- predict(svm_model, testData)
    # Evaluate model performance
    confusionMatrix(predictions, testData$Species)
```

6. **Apply Random Forest for Classification**: Utilize the random forest algorithm to build an ensemble classifier. Analyze feature importance to understand which variables contribute most to the predictions.

R

```
    library(randomForest)
    library(caret)
```

```r
# Load dataset
data(iris)
# Split data into training and testing sets
set.seed(123)
trainIndex <- createDataPartition(iris$Species, p = 0.7, list =
FALSE)
trainData <- iris[trainIndex, ]
testData  <- iris[-trainIndex, ]
# Train random forest model
rf_model <- randomForest(Species ~ ., data = trainData,
importance = TRUE)
# Predict on test data
predictions <- predict(rf_model, testData)
# Evaluate model performance
confusionMatrix(predictions, testData$Species)
# Plot feature importance
varImpPlot(rf_model)
```

7. **Develop a Gradient Boosting Model**: Implement gradient boosting to improve prediction accuracy. Tune hyperparameters to optimize model performance.

R

```r
library(gbm)
library(caret)
# Load dataset
data(iris)
# Convert Species to numeric for gbm
iris$SpeciesNumeric <- as.numeric(iris$Species) - 1
# Split data into training and testing sets
set.seed(123)
trainIndex <- createDataPartition(iris$SpeciesNumeric, p = 0.7,
list = FALSE)
trainData <- iris[trainIndex, ]
```

```r
    testData  <- iris[-trainIndex, ]
    # Train gradient boosting model
    gbm_model <- gbm(SpeciesNumeric ~ Sepal.Length + Sepal.Width +
Petal.Length + Petal.Width,
                     data = trainData, distribution =
"multinomial",
                     n.trees = 100, interaction.depth = 3,
shrinkage = 0.1, cv.folds = 5)
    # Determine optimal number of trees
    best_iter <- gbm.perf(gbm_model, method = "cv")
    # Predict on test data
    predictions <- predict(gbm_model, testData, n.trees =
best_iter, type = "response")
    predicted_classes <- apply(predictions, 1, which.max)
    predicted_species <- factor(predicted_classes, labels =
levels(iris$Species))
    # Evaluate model performance
    confusionMatrix(predicted_species, testData$Species)
```

8. **Implement k-Means Clustering**: Apply k-means clustering to identify natural groupings within your data. Determine the optimal number of clusters using the Elbow method.

R

```r
    library(ggplot2)
    # Load dataset
    data(iris)
    # Select numerical features
    numeric_data <- iris[, -5]
    # Determine optimal number of clusters using Elbow method
    wss <- sapply(1:10, function(k){
       kmeans(numeric_data, centers = k, nstart = 10)$tot.withinss
    })
    # Plot the Elbow curve
```

```r
    plot(1:10, wss, type = "b", pch = 19, frame = FALSE,
         xlab = "Number of clusters K",
         ylab = "Total within-clusters sum of squares")
    # Apply k-means with k = 3
    set.seed(123)
    kmeans_result <- kmeans(numeric_data, centers = 3, nstart = 25)
    # Add cluster assignment to the dataset
    iris$Cluster <- as.factor(kmeans_result$cluster)
    # Visualize the clusters
    ggplot(iris, aes(x = Sepal.Length, y = Sepal.Width, color =
Cluster)) +
        geom_point(size = 2) +
        labs(title = "k-Means Clustering of Iris Dataset") +
        theme_minimal()
```

9. **Perform Hierarchical Clustering**: Execute hierarchical clustering to explore the structure of your data. Visualize the dendrogram to interpret the hierarchical relationships between observations.

R

```r
    library(ggplot2)
    library(cluster)
    # Load dataset
    data(iris)
    # Select numerical features
    numeric_data <- scale(iris[, -5])
    # Compute distance matrix
    distance_matrix <- dist(numeric_data, method = "euclidean")
    # Perform hierarchical clustering
    hc <- hclust(distance_matrix, method = "ward.D2")
    # Plot dendrogram
    plot(hc, labels = iris$Species, main = "Hierarchical Clustering
Dendrogram", xlab = "", sub = "")
```

```
# Cut the tree into 3 clusters
clusters <- cutree(hc, k = 3)
# Add cluster assignments to the dataset
iris$HC_Cluster <- as.factor(clusters)
# Visualize the clusters
ggplot(iris, aes(x = Sepal.Length, y = Sepal.Width, color =
HC_Cluster)) +
    geom_point(size = 2) +
    labs(title = "Hierarchical Clustering of Iris Dataset") +
    theme_minimal()
```

10. **Develop a Naive Bayes Classifier**: Create a Naive Bayes model to classify data points based on feature probabilities. Evaluate the model's accuracy and interpret the results.

R

```
library(e1071)
library(caret)
# Load dataset
data(iris)
# Split data into training and testing sets
set.seed(123)
trainIndex <- createDataPartition(iris$Species, p = 0.7, list =
FALSE)
trainData <- iris[trainIndex, ]
testData  <- iris[-trainIndex, ]
# Train Naive Bayes model
nb_model <- naiveBayes(Species ~ ., data = trainData)
# Predict on test data
predictions <- predict(nb_model, testData)
# Evaluate model performance
confusionMatrix(predictions, testData$Species)
```

11. Implement a Neural Network for Classification: Use the nnet package to build a simple neural network model for classifying data points. Adjust the size of hidden layers to optimize performance.

R

```
library(nnet)
library(caret)
# Load dataset
data(iris)
# Split data into training and testing sets
set.seed(123)
trainIndex <- createDataPartition(iris$Species, p = 0.7, list = FALSE)
trainData <- iris[trainIndex, ]
testData  <- iris[-trainIndex, ]
# Train neural network model
nn_model <- nnet(Species ~ ., data = trainData, size = 3, decay = 0.1, maxit = 200)
# Predict on test data
predictions <- predict(nn_model, testData, type = "class")
# Evaluate model performance
confusionMatrix(predictions, testData$Species)
```

12. Apply Gradient Boosting Machines (GBM): Utilize the gbm package to train a gradient boosting model. Fine-tune the number of trees and interaction depth to enhance model accuracy.

R

```
library(gbm)
library(caret)
# Load dataset
data(iris)
# Split data into training and testing sets
set.seed(123)
```

```r
    trainIndex <- createDataPartition(iris$Species, p = 0.7, list =
FALSE)

    trainData <- iris[trainIndex, ]

    testData  <- iris[-trainIndex, ]

    # Train GBM model

    gbm_model <- gbm(Species ~ ., data = trainData, distribution =
"multinomial",

                       n.trees = 100, interaction.depth = 3,
shrinkage = 0.1, cv.folds = 5)

    # Determine optimal number of trees

    best_iter <- gbm.perf(gbm_model, method = "cv")

    # Predict on test data

    predictions <- predict(gbm_model, testData, n.trees =
best_iter, type = "response")

    predicted_classes <- apply(predictions, 1, which.max)

    predicted_species <- factor(predicted_classes, labels =
levels(iris$Species))

    # Evaluate model performance

    confusionMatrix(predicted_species, testData$Species)
```

13. **Conduct Cross-Validation for Model Evaluation**: Implement k-fold cross-validation to assess the reliability of your machine learning models. Compare performance metrics across different folds.

R

```r
    library(caret)

    # Load dataset

    data(iris)

    # Define cross-validation method

    ctrl <- trainControl(method = "cv", number = 5)

    # Train a Support Vector Machine model with cross-validation

    set.seed(123)

    svm_model <- train(Species ~ ., data = iris, method =
"svmRadial",
```

```
                      trControl = ctrl, preProcess = c("center",
"scale"),
                         tuneLength = 8)
   # Display model results
   print(svm_model)
   # Plot cross-validation results
   plot(svm_model)
```

14. **Evaluate Model Performance with ROC Curves**: Generate ROC curves to visualize the trade-off between sensitivity and specificity for your classification models. Calculate the Area Under the Curve (AUC) as a performance metric.

R

```
   library(pROC)
   library(caret)
   # Load dataset
   data(iris)
   # Convert Species to binary outcome
   iris$SpeciesBinary <- ifelse(iris$Species == "setosa", "Yes",
"No")
   # Split data into training and testing sets
   set.seed(123)
   trainIndex <- createDataPartition(iris$SpeciesBinary, p = 0.7,
list = FALSE)
   trainData <- iris[trainIndex, ]
   testData  <- iris[-trainIndex, ]
   # Train logistic regression model
   model <- glm(SpeciesBinary ~ Sepal.Length + Sepal.Width +
Petal.Length + Petal.Width,
               data = trainData, family = binomial)
   # Predict probabilities
   probabilities <- predict(model, testData, type = "response")
   # Generate ROC curve
   roc_obj <- roc(testData$SpeciesBinary, probabilities)
```

```r
plot(roc_obj, main = "ROC Curve for Logistic Regression Model")
auc(roc_obj)
```

15. **Identify and Handle Overfitting with Regularization**: Train a machine learning model with regularization techniques such as Lasso or Ridge regression to prevent overfitting. Compare its performance with an unregularized model.

R

```r
library(glmnet)
library(caret)
# Load dataset
data(iris)
# Convert Species to binary outcome
iris$SpeciesBinary <- ifelse(iris$Species == "setosa", 1, 0)
# Prepare data for glmnet
x <- model.matrix(SpeciesBinary ~ Sepal.Length + Sepal.Width +
Petal.Length + Petal.Width, data = iris)[, -1]
y <- iris$SpeciesBinary
# Split data into training and testing sets
set.seed(123)
trainIndex <- createDataPartition(y, p = 0.7, list = FALSE)
x_train <- x[trainIndex, ]
y_train <- y[trainIndex]
x_test  <- x[-trainIndex, ]
y_test  <- y[-trainIndex]
# Train Lasso model
lasso_model <- cv.glmnet(x_train, y_train, alpha = 1, family =
"binomial")
# Predict on test data
predictions <- predict(lasso_model, newx = x_test, s =
"lambda.min", type = "response")
predicted_classes <- ifelse(predictions > 0.5, 1, 0)
```

```r
# Evaluate model performance
confusionMatrix(as.factor(predicted_classes),
as.factor(y_test))
```

16. **Apply Ensemble Learning Techniques**: Combine multiple machine learning models to create an ensemble that improves prediction accuracy. Use techniques such as bagging or boosting to enhance model performance.

R

```r
library(caret)
library(randomForest)
# Load dataset
data(iris)
# Split data into training and testing sets
set.seed(123)
trainIndex <- createDataPartition(iris$Species, p = 0.7, list = FALSE)
trainData <- iris[trainIndex, ]
testData  <- iris[-trainIndex, ]
# Train individual models
rf_model <- train(Species ~ ., data = trainData, method = "rf", trControl = trainControl(method = "cv", number = 5))
svm_model <- train(Species ~ ., data = trainData, method = "svmRadial", trControl = trainControl(method = "cv", number = 5))
# Combine predictions using majority voting
rf_predictions <- predict(rf_model, testData)
svm_predictions <- predict(svm_model, testData)
ensemble_predictions <- factor(ifelse(rf_predictions == svm_predictions, as.character(rf_predictions), "setosa"),
                               levels = levels(iris$Species))
# Evaluate ensemble model performance
confusionMatrix(ensemble_predictions, testData$Species)
```

17. **Optimize Hyperparameters with Grid Search**: Perform a grid search to find the optimal hyperparameters for your machine learning model. Utilize cross-validation to ensure robustness during the search process.

R

```r
library(caret)
# Load dataset
data(iris)
# Split data into training and testing sets
set.seed(123)
trainIndex <- createDataPartition(iris$Species, p = 0.7, list = FALSE)
trainData <- iris[trainIndex, ]
testData  <- iris[-trainIndex, ]
# Define training control with grid search
ctrl <- trainControl(method = "cv", number = 5, search = "grid")
# Define grid of hyperparameters
grid <- expand.grid(.mtry = c(2, 3, 4))
# Train Random Forest model with grid search
rf_model <- train(Species ~ ., data = trainData, method = "rf",
                  trControl = ctrl, tuneGrid = grid, importance = TRUE)
# Display best hyperparameters
print(rf_model$bestTune)
# Predict on test data
predictions <- predict(rf_model, testData)
# Evaluate model performance
confusionMatrix(predictions, testData$Species)
```

18. **Analyze Feature Importance**: Determine which features contribute most to your machine learning model's predictions. Use feature importance scores to gain insights into the underlying data patterns.

R

```r
library(randomForest)
library(caret)
# Load dataset
data(iris)
# Train Random Forest model
set.seed(123)
rf_model <- randomForest(Species ~ ., data = iris, importance =
TRUE)
# Display feature importance
importance(rf_model)
varImpPlot(rf_model)
```

19. **Implement Cross-Validation for Model Selection**: Compare multiple machine learning models using cross-validation to identify the best-performing model for your dataset.

R

```r
library(caret)
# Load dataset
data(iris)
# Define cross-validation method
ctrl <- trainControl(method = "cv", number = 5)
# Define models to compare
models <- c("rf", "svmRadial", "nnet")
# Train and compare models
set.seed(123)
model_list <- lapply(models, function(model){
    train(Species ~ ., data = iris, method = model, trControl =
ctrl, tuneLength = 5)
})
names(model_list) <- models
# Compare model performances
```

```r
resamples <- resamples(model_list)
summary(resamples)
dotplot(resamples)
```

20. **Deploy a Machine Learning Model with Shiny**: Create a Shiny application that allows users to input data and receive predictions from your trained machine learning model in real-time.

R

```r
library(shiny)
library(randomForest)
# Train model on iris dataset
data(iris)
rf_model <- randomForest(Species ~ ., data = iris)
# Define UI
ui <- fluidPage(
  titlePanel("Iris Species Prediction"),
  sidebarLayout(
    sidebarPanel(
      numericInput("sepal_length", "Sepal Length:", value =
5.5),
      numericInput("sepal_width", "Sepal Width:", value = 3.0),
      numericInput("petal_length", "Petal Length:", value =
4.5),
      numericInput("petal_width", "Petal Width:", value = 1.5),
      actionButton("predict_btn", "Predict Species")
    ),
    mainPanel(
      verbatimTextOutput("prediction")
    )
  )
)
# Define server logic
```

```r
server <- function(input, output) {
  observeEvent(input$predict_btn, {
    new_data <- data.frame(
      Sepal.Length = input$sepal_length,
      Sepal.Width = input$sepal_width,
      Petal.Length = input$petal_length,
      Petal.Width = input$petal_width
    )
    pred <- predict(rf_model, new_data)
    output$prediction <- renderText({
      paste("Predicted Species:", as.character(pred))
    })
  })
}
# Run the application
shinyApp(ui = ui, server = server)
```

These exercises encompass a broad range of machine learning techniques, providing hands-on experience with model building, evaluation, and deployment using R. Engage with each exercise to deepen your understanding and proficiency in applying machine learning methods to real-world data.</h3>

Shiny Application Development Exercises

1. **Create a Basic Shiny App**: Develop your first simple Shiny application that displays a static plot. This exercise will familiarize you with the fundamental structure of a Shiny app, including the `ui` and `server` components.

R

```r
library(shiny)
ui <- fluidPage(
  titlePanel("Basic Shiny App"),
  sidebarLayout(
```

```r
    sidebarPanel(),
    mainPanel(
      plotOutput("basicPlot")
    )
  )
)
server <- function(input, output) {
  output$basicPlot <- renderPlot({
    plot(mtcars$wt, mtcars$mpg,
         main = "Car Weight vs. MPG",
         xlab = "Weight (1000 lbs)",
         ylab = "Miles Per Gallon",
         pch = 19, col = "blue")
  })
}
shinyApp(ui = ui, server = server)
```

2. **Add User Inputs to Your Shiny App**: Enhance the basic app by adding input controls, such as sliders, to allow users to interactively filter the data displayed in the plot.

R

```r
library(shiny)
ui <- fluidPage(
  titlePanel("Interactive Shiny App"),
  sidebarLayout(
    sidebarPanel(
      sliderInput("wtRange", "Weight Range:",
                  min = min(mtcars$wt),
                  max = max(mtcars$wt),
                  value = c(min(mtcars$wt), max(mtcars$wt)),
                  step = 0.1)
    ),
```

```r
    mainPanel(
      plotOutput("interactivePlot")
    )
  )
)
server <- function(input, output) {
  output$interactivePlot <- renderPlot({
    filtered_data <- subset(mtcars, wt >= input$wtRange<a
href="https://shinyapps.io/">1] & wt <= input$wtRange[2])
    plot(filtered_data$wt, filtered_data$mpg,
        main = "Filtered Car Weight vs. MPG",
        xlab = "Weight (1000 lbs)",
        ylab = "Miles Per Gallon",
        pch = 19, col = "green")
  })
}
shinyApp(ui = ui, server = server)
```

3. **Implement Reactive Expressions**: Use reactive expressions to optimize your Shiny app's performance by preventing unnecessary re-computations when inputs change.

R

```r
library(shiny)
ui <- fluidPage(
  titlePanel("Reactive Expressions in Shiny"),
  sidebarLayout(
    sidebarPanel(
      sliderInput("hpRange", "Horsepower Range:",
                  min = min(mtcars$hp),
                  max = max(mtcars$hp),
                  value = c(min(mtcars$hp), max(mtcars$hp)),
                  step = 10)
    ),
```

```r
    mainPanel(
        plotOutput("reactivePlot"),
        tableOutput("dataTable")
    )
  )
)
server <- function(input, output) {
  filteredData <- reactive({
    subset(mtcars, hp >= input$hpRange[1] & hp <=
input$hpRange[2])
  })
  output$reactivePlot <- renderPlot({
    plot(filteredData()$hp, filteredData()$mpg,
         main = "Horsepower vs. MPG",
         xlab = "Horsepower",
         ylab = "Miles Per Gallon",
         pch = 19, col = "purple")
  })
  output$dataTable <- renderTable({
    filteredData()
  })
}
shinyApp(ui = ui, server = server)
```

4. Incorporate Select Inputs for Dynamic Filtering: Add dropdown menus using selectInput() to allow users to filter data based on categorical variables, such as the number of cylinders in cars.

R

```r
library(shiny)
ui <- fluidPage(
  titlePanel("Select Input for Dynamic Filtering"),
  sidebarLayout(
```

```r
        sidebarPanel(
          selectInput("cylSelect", "Select Cylinders:",
                      choices = sort(unique(mtcars$cyl)),
                      selected = unique(mtcars$cyl),
                      multiple = TRUE)
        ),
        mainPanel(
          plotOutput("selectPlot")
        )
      )
    )
    server <- function(input, output) {
      output$selectPlot <- renderPlot({
        filtered_data <- subset(mtcars, cyl %in% input$cylSelect)
        plot(filtered_data$wt, filtered_data$mpg,
             main = "Weight vs. MPG by Cylinders",
             xlab = "Weight (1000 lbs)",
             ylab = "Miles Per Gallon",
             pch = 19,
             col = as.factor(filtered_data$cyl))
        legend("topright", legend = unique(filtered_data$cyl),
                col = unique(as.factor(filtered_data$cyl)), pch =
19, title = "Cylinders")
      })
    }
    shinyApp(ui = ui, server = server)
```

5. **Create Reactive Text Outputs**: Display dynamic textual information that updates based on user inputs. For example, show the average MPG of the filtered dataset.

R

```r
    library(shiny)
    ui <- fluidPage(
```

```r
    titlePanel("Reactive Text Outputs"),
    sidebarLayout(
      sidebarPanel(
        sliderInput("dispRange", "Displacement Range:",
                    min = min(mtcars$disp),
                    max = max(mtcars$disp),
                    value = c(min(mtcars$disp),
max(mtcars$disp)),
                    step = 50)
      ),
      mainPanel(
        plotOutput("dispPlot"),
        textOutput("avgMpg")
      )
    )
  )
  server <- function(input, output) {
    filteredData <- reactive({
      subset(mtcars, disp >= input$dispRange[1] & disp <=
input$dispRange[2])
    })
    output$dispPlot <- renderPlot({
      plot(filteredData()$disp, filteredData()$mpg,
           main = "Displacement vs. MPG",
           xlab = "Displacement (cu.in.)",
           ylab = "Miles Per Gallon",
           pch = 19, col = "darkred")
    })
    output$avgMpg <- renderText({
      avg <- mean(filteredData()$mpg)
      paste("Average MPG:", round(avg, 2))
    })
```

```r
  }
  shinyApp(ui = ui, server = server)
```

6. **Develop a Shiny App with Multiple Tabs**: Organize your Shiny application into multiple tabs using `tabsetPanel()` to segregate different functionalities or visualizations.

R

```r
  library(shiny)
  ui <- fluidPage(
    titlePanel("Shiny App with Multiple Tabs"),
    sidebarLayout(
      sidebarPanel(
        sliderInput("hpRange", "Horsepower Range:",
                    min = min(mtcars$hp),
                    max = max(mtcars$hp),
                    value = c(min(mtcars$hp), max(mtcars$hp)),
                    step = 10)
      ),
      mainPanel(
        tabsetPanel(
          tabPanel("Plot", plotOutput("multiTabPlot")),
          tabPanel("Summary", verbatimTextOutput("dataSummary")),
          tabPanel("Data", tableOutput("dataTable"))
        )
      )
    )
  )
  server <- function(input, output) {
    filteredData <- reactive({
      subset(mtcars, hp >= input$hpRange[1] & hp <=
input$hpRange[2])
    })
    output$multiTabPlot <- renderPlot({
```

```r
    plot(filteredData()$wt, filteredData()$mpg,
         main = "Filtered Weight vs. MPG",
         xlab = "Weight (1000 lbs)",
         ylab = "Miles Per Gallon",
         pch = 19, col = "brown")
  })
  output$dataSummary <- renderPrint({
    summary(filteredData())
  })
  output$dataTable <- renderTable({
    filteredData()
  })
}
shinyApp(ui = ui, server = server)
```

7. **Integrate ggplot2 Visualizations in Shiny**: Utilize the power of `ggplot2` within your Shiny app to create more advanced and customizable plots.

R

```r
library(shiny)
library(ggplot2)
ui <- fluidPage(
  titlePanel("ggplot2 in Shiny"),
  sidebarLayout(
    sidebarPanel(
      selectInput("colorVar", "Select Variable for Color:",
                  choices = names(mtcars)[sapply(mtcars,
is.numeric)],
                  selected = "hp")
    ),
    mainPanel(
      plotOutput("ggPlot")
    )
```

```r
    )
  )
  server <- function(input, output) {
    output$ggPlot <- renderPlot({
      ggplot(mtcars, aes(x = wt, y = mpg, color
= .data[[input$colorVar]])) +
        geom_point(size = 3) +
        scale_color_gradient(low = "yellow", high = "red") +
        labs(title = "Weight vs. MPG with ggplot2",
             x = "Weight (1000 lbs)",
             y = "Miles Per Gallon",
             color = input$colorVar) +
        theme_minimal()
    })
  }
  shinyApp(ui = ui, server = server)
```

8. **Add Download Buttons for Data and Plots**: Empower users to download the filtered dataset or generated plots directly from the Shiny application using downloadButton() and downloadHandler().

R

```r
  library(shiny)
  ui <- fluidPage(
    titlePanel("Download Functionality in Shiny"),
    sidebarLayout(
      sidebarPanel(
        sliderInput("mpgRange", "Miles Per Gallon Range:",
                    min = min(mtcars$mpg),
                    max = max(mtcars$mpg),
                    value = c(min(mtcars$mpg), max(mtcars$mpg)),
                    step = 1),
        downloadButton("downloadData", "Download Data"),
```

```r
        downloadButton("downloadPlot", "Download Plot")
      ),
      mainPanel(
        plotOutput("downloadPlotOutput"),
        tableOutput("filteredTable")
      )
    )
  )
  server <- function(input, output) {
    filteredData <- reactive({
      subset(mtcars, mpg >= input$mpgRange[1] & mpg <=
input$mpgRange[2])
    })
    output$downloadData <- downloadHandler(
      filename = function() {
        paste("filtered_data_", Sys.Date(), ".csv", sep = "")
      },
      content = function(file) {
        write.csv(filteredData(), file, row.names = FALSE)
      }
    )
    output$downloadPlot <- downloadHandler(
      filename = function() {
        paste("mpg_plot_", Sys.Date(), ".png", sep = "")
      },
      content = function(file) {
        png(file)
        plot(filteredData()$wt, filteredData()$mpg,
             main = "MPG vs. Weight",
             xlab = "Weight (1000 lbs)",
             ylab = "Miles Per Gallon",
             pch = 19, col = "darkgreen")
```

```r
      dev.off()
    }
  )
  output$downloadPlotOutput <- renderPlot({
    plot(filteredData()$wt, filteredData()$mpg,
         main = "MPG vs. Weight",
         xlab = "Weight (1000 lbs)",
         ylab = "Miles Per Gallon",
         pch = 19, col = "darkgreen")
  })
  output$filteredTable <- renderTable({
    filteredData()
  })
}
shinyApp(ui = ui, server = server)
```

9. **Incorporate Reactive Values and Observers**: Utilize reactive values and observers to manage and respond to changes within your Shiny app, enabling dynamic and responsive interactions.

R

```r
  library(shiny)
  ui <- fluidPage(
    titlePanel("Reactive Values and Observers"),
    sidebarLayout(
      sidebarPanel(
        actionButton("increment", "Increment Counter"),
        actionButton("reset", "Reset Counter")
      ),
      mainPanel(
        textOutput("counterValue")
      )
```

```
      )
    )
    server <- function(input, output, session) {
      rv <- reactiveValues(counter = 0)
      observeEvent(input$increment, {
        rv$counter <- rv$counter + 1
      })
      observeEvent(input$reset, {
        rv$counter <- 0
      })
      output$counterValue <- renderText({
        paste("Counter Value:", rv$counter)
      })
    }
    shinyApp(ui = ui, server = server)
```

10. **Embed External HTML Content**: Integrate external HTML elements or widgets into your Shiny app using HTML tags and `htmlOutput()`. This allows for the inclusion of rich content beyond standard Shiny components.

R

```
    library(shiny)
    ui <- fluidPage(
      titlePanel("Embedding External HTML Content"),
      sidebarLayout(
        sidebarPanel(),
        mainPanel(
          htmlOutput("externalHTML")
        )
      )
    )
    server <- function(input, output) {
```

```r
    output$externalHTML <- renderUI({
      HTML("
        <h2>Welcome to the Shiny App</h2>
        <p>This paragraph is <strong>bold</strong> and
<em>italicized</em>.</p>
        <a href='https://www.r-project.org/'
target='_blank'>Visit the R Project</a>
      ")
    })
  }
  shinyApp(ui = ui, server = server)
```

11. **Use Conditional Panels for Dynamic UI Elements**: Display or hide UI components based on user inputs using `conditionalPanel()`. This technique enhances user experience by showing relevant options only when necessary.

R

```r
  library(shiny)
  ui <- fluidPage(
    titlePanel("Conditional Panels in Shiny"),
    sidebarLayout(
      sidebarPanel(
        checkboxInput("showPlot", "Show Plot", value = TRUE),
        conditionalPanel(
          condition = "input.showPlot == true",
          sliderInput("pointSize", "Point Size:",
                      min = 1, max = 10, value = 3)
        )
      ),
      mainPanel(
        conditionalPanel(
          condition = "input.showPlot == true",
          plotOutput("conditionalPlot")
```

236

```
        ),
        conditionalPanel(
          condition = "input.showPlot == false",
          h4("Plot is hidden. Check the box to display the
plot.")
        )
      )
    )
  )
  server <- function(input, output) {
    output$conditionalPlot <- renderPlot({
      plot(mtcars$wt, mtcars$mpg,
           main = "Conditional Plot Display",
           xlab = "Weight (1000 lbs)",
           ylab = "Miles Per Gallon",
           pch = 19, col = "orange",
           cex = input$pointSize)
    })
  }
  shinyApp(ui = ui, server = server)
```

12. **Implement Data Tables with DT Package**: Enhance your Shiny app by integrating interactive data tables using the DT package, allowing users to search, sort, and paginate through data efficiently.

R

```
library(shiny)
library(DT)
ui <- fluidPage(
  titlePanel("Interactive Data Tables with DT"),
  sidebarLayout(
    sidebarPanel(
      selectInput("gearSelect", "Select Gears:",
```

```r
                    choices = sort(unique(mtcars$gear)),
                    selected = unique(mtcars$gear),
                    multiple = TRUE)
      ),
      mainPanel(
        DTOutput("dataTable")
      )
    )
  )
)
server <- function(input, output) {
  output$dataTable <- renderDT({
    filtered_data <- subset(mtcars, gear %in% input$gearSelect)
    datatable(filtered_data, options = list(pageLength = 5),
              caption = 'Filtered MTCARS Dataset')
  })
}
shinyApp(ui = ui, server = server)
```

13. **Create Interactive Maps with Leaflet**: Incorporate geospatial data visualizations into your Shiny app using the `leaflet` package. Display interactive maps with markers based on dataset coordinates.

R

```r
library(shiny)
library(leaflet)
# Sample dataset with coordinates
locations <- data.frame(
    name = c("New York", "Los Angeles", "Chicago", "Houston",
"Phoenix"),
   lat = c(40.7128, 34.0522, 41.8781, 29.7604, 33.4484),
   lon = c(-74.0060, -118.2437, -87.6298, -95.3698, -112.0740)
)
ui <- fluidPage(
```

```r
      titlePanel("Interactive Maps with Leaflet"),
      sidebarLayout(
        sidebarPanel(
          checkboxGroupInput("cities", "Select Cities:",
                            choices = locations$name,
                            selected = locations$name)
        ),
        mainPanel(
          leafletOutput("map")
        )
      )
    )
  server <- function(input, output) {
    output$map <- renderLeaflet({
      leaflet(data = locations) %>%
        addTiles() %>%
        setView(lng = -96.9, lat = 37.8, zoom = 4)
    })
    observe({
      proxy <- leafletProxy("map", data = locations)
      proxy %>% clearMarkers()
      selected <- subset(locations, name %in% input$cities)
      proxy %>% addMarkers(~lon, ~lat, popup = ~name)
    })
  }
  shinyApp(ui = ui, server = server)
```

14. Develop a Shiny App with Reactive Data Uploading: Allow users to upload their own datasets and perform dynamic analyses or visualizations based on the uploaded data.

R

```r
    library(shiny)
```

239

```r
    library(ggplot2)
    ui <- fluidPage(
      titlePanel("Reactive Data Uploading"),
      sidebarLayout(
        sidebarPanel(
          fileInput("fileUpload", "Upload CSV File",
                    accept = c("text/csv",
                               "text/comma-separated-values,text/
plain",
                               ".csv")),
          uiOutput("xSelect"),
          uiOutput("ySelect")
        ),
        mainPanel(
          plotOutput("uploadedPlot"),
          tableOutput("uploadedTable")
        )
      )
    )
    server <- function(input, output, session) {
      uploadedData <- reactive({
        req(input$fileUpload)
        read.csv(input$fileUpload$datapath, stringsAsFactors =
FALSE)
      })
      output$xSelect <- renderUI({
        req(uploadedData())
        selectInput("xVar", "Select X-axis Variable:",
                    choices = names(uploadedData()),
                    selected = names(uploadedData())[1])
      })
      output$ySelect <- renderUI({
```

```r
    req(uploadedData())
    selectInput("yVar", "Select Y-axis Variable:",
                choices = names(uploadedData()),
                selected = names(uploadedData())[2])
  })
  output$uploadedPlot <- renderPlot({
    req(input$xVar, input$yVar)
    ggplot(uploadedData(), aes_string(x = input$xVar, y =
input$yVar)) +
        geom_point(color = "darkblue") +
        labs(title = "Uploaded Data Plot",
            x = input$xVar,
            y = input$yVar) +
        theme_minimal()
  })
  output$uploadedTable <- renderTable({
    uploadedData()
  })
}
shinyApp(ui = ui, server = server)
```

15. Incorporate Authentication in Shiny Apps: Secure your Shiny application by adding user authentication, ensuring that only authorized users can access certain features or data.

R

```r
library(shiny)
library(shinyauthr)
library(dplyr)
# Sample user credentials
user_base <- data.frame(
  user = c("user1", "user2"),
  password = c("password1", "password2"),
```

```r
    stringsAsFactors = FALSE
)
ui <- fluidPage(
  shinyauthr::loginUI("login"),
  uiOutput("appUI")
)
server <- function(input, output, session) {
  credentials <- shinyauthr::loginServer(
    "login",
    data = user_base,
    user_col = user,
    pwd_col = password,
    log_out = reactive(logout_init())
  )
  logout_init <- shinyauthr::logoutServer("logout")
  output$appUI <- renderUI({
    req(credentials()$user_auth)
    fluidPage(
      titlePanel("Secure Shiny App"),
      sidebarLayout(
        sidebarPanel(
          shinyauthr::logoutUI("logout")
        ),
        mainPanel(
          h3(paste("Welcome,", credentials()$info$user)),
          plotOutput("securePlot")
        )
      )
    )
  })
  output$securePlot <- renderPlot({
    plot(mtcars$hp, mtcars$mpg,
```

```r
            main = "Secure Plot Access",
            xlab = "Horsepower",
            ylab = "Miles Per Gallon",
            pch = 19, col = "navy")
    })
  }
  shinyApp(ui = ui, server = server)
```

16. **Use Reactive Polling for Real-Time Data Updates**: Implement reactive polling to fetch and display real-time data updates within your Shiny app, enabling dynamic data monitoring.

R

```r
    library(shiny)
    ui <- fluidPage(
      titlePanel("Real-Time Data Updates with Reactive Polling"),
      sidebarLayout(
        sidebarPanel(
          actionButton("refresh", "Refresh Data")
        ),
        mainPanel(
          tableOutput("realTimeTable"),
          textOutput("lastUpdated")
        )
      )
    )
    server <- function(input, output, session) {
      lastUpdated <- reactiveVal(Sys.time())
      dataValue <- reactivePoll(1000, session,
                                  checkFunc = function() { Sys.time()
},
                                  valueFunc = function() {
                                    head(mtcars, 5)
```

```r
                                   })
  output$realTimeTable <- renderTable({
    dataValue()
  })
  output$lastUpdated <- renderText({
    paste("Last Updated:", lastUpdated())
  })
  observeEvent(input$refresh, {
    lastUpdated(Sys.time())
  })
}
shinyApp(ui = ui, server = server)
```

17. **Integrate Shiny Modules for Reusability**: Organize your Shiny app into modules to promote code reusability and better structure, especially for complex applications.

R

```r
library(shiny)
# Define UI for a module
plotModuleUI <- function(id) {
  ns <- NS(id)
  tagList(
    plotOutput(ns("plot"))
  )
}
# Define server logic for a module
plotModule <- function(input, output, session, data, x, y) {
  output$plot <- renderPlot({
    plot(data[[x]], data[[y]],
         main = paste("Plot of", x, "vs", y),
         xlab = x,
         ylab = y,
```

```r
                pch = 19, col = "teal")
    })
  }
  ui <- fluidPage(
    titlePanel("Shiny Modules Example"),
    sidebarLayout(
      sidebarPanel(
        selectInput("xVar", "X-axis Variable:",
                    choices = names(mtcars),
                    selected = "wt"),
        selectInput("yVar", "Y-axis Variable:",
                    choices = names(mtcars),
                    selected = "mpg")
      ),
      mainPanel(
        plotModuleUI("module1")
      )
    )
  )
  server <- function(input, output, session) {
    callModule(plotModule, "module1",
               data = mtcars,
               x = reactive(input$xVar),
               y = reactive(input$yVar))
  }
  shinyApp(ui = ui, server = server)
```

18. Customize Shiny App Themes with shinythemes: Enhance the aesthetic appeal of your Shiny app by applying different themes using the shinythemes package.

R

```r
  library(shiny)
```

```r
library(shinythemes)
ui <- fluidPage(
  theme = shinytheme("cerulean"),
  titlePanel("Shiny App with Customized Theme"),
  sidebarLayout(
    sidebarPanel(
      sliderInput("bins", "Number of Bins:",
                  min = 1, max = 50, value = 30)
    ),
    mainPanel(
      plotOutput("histPlot")
    )
  )
)
server <- function(input, output) {
  output$histPlot <- renderPlot({
    x <- faithful$waiting
    bins <- seq(min(x), max(x), length.out = input$bins + 1)
    hist(x, breaks = bins, col = "darkgray",
         border = "white", main = "Histogram of Waiting Times",
         xlab = "Waiting time to next eruption (in mins)")
  })
}
shinyApp(ui = ui, server = server)
```

19. **Add Interactive Widgets with Shiny Widgets Package**: Incorporate advanced interactive widgets from the `shinyWidgets` package to enhance user interaction and functionality within your app.

R

```r
library(shiny)
library(shinyWidgets)
ui <- fluidPage(
```

```r
    titlePanel("Interactive Widgets with shinyWidgets"),
    sidebarLayout(
      sidebarPanel(
        pickerInput("selectCyl", "Select Cylinders:",
                    choices = sort(unique(mtcars$cyl)),
                    selected = unique(mtcars$cyl),
                    multiple = TRUE,
                    options = list(actions-box = TRUE))
      ),
      mainPanel(
        plotOutput("widgetPlot")
      )
    )
)
server <- function(input, output) {
  output$widgetPlot <- renderPlot({
    filtered_data <- subset(mtcars, cyl %in% input$selectCyl)
    boxplot(mpg ~ cyl, data = filtered_data,
            main = "MPG by Number of Cylinders",
            xlab = "Cylinders",
            ylab = "Miles Per Gallon",
            col = "lightblue")
  })
}
shinyApp(ui = ui, server = server)
```

20. **Deploy Your Shiny App to the Web**: Learn how to deploy your Shiny application online using platforms like [ShinyApps.io, making it accessible to a broader audience.

R

```r
# Install the rsconnect package if not already installed
# install.packages("rsconnect")
library(rsconnect)
# Set your ShinyApps.io account details
```

```
rsconnect::setAccountInfo(name='yourname',
                          token='yourtoken',
                          secret='yoursecret')
# Deploy the Shiny app
rsconnect::deployApp('path/to/your/app')
```

These exercises guide you through various aspects of developing Shiny applications, from basic setups to more advanced functionalities like user authentication and real-time data updates. By working through these tasks, you'll build a strong foundation in Shiny app development, enabling you to create dynamic and interactive data-driven web applications.

Package Development Exercises

1. Set Up Your Package Structure

- Install and load the necessary packages:

r

```
install.packages("devtools")
install.packages("usethis")
library(devtools)
library(usethis)
```

- Create a new package:

r

```
usethis::create_package("path/to/your/packageName")
```

- Navigate to the package directory:

r

```
setwd("path/to/your/packageName")
```

2. Define Functions

- Create a new R script for your functions:

```r
    usethis::use_r("functionName")
```

- Inside the created `R/functionName.R` file, define your function:

```r
    #' Title of Your Function
    #'
    #' Description of what your function does.
    #'
    #' @param param1 Description of parameter 1
    #' @param param2 Description of parameter 2
    #' @return Description of the return value
    #' @export
    functionName <- function(param1, param2) {
        # Function implementation}
```

3. Document Your Package

- Use `roxygen2` to generate documentation:

```r
    devtools::document()
```

- This will create the necessary `.Rd` files in the `man/` directory based on the comments in your functions.

4. Add Dependencies

- Specify package dependencies in the DESCRIPTION file:

```r
    usethis::use_package("dplyr")
    usethis::use_package("ggplot2")
```

- This ensures that your package will automatically install these dependencies when someone installs your package.

5. Include Tests

- Set up testing infrastructure:

r

```
usethis::use_testthat()
```

- Create a test file for your function:

r

```
usethis::use_test("functionName")
```

- In the `tests/testthat/test-functionName.R` file, write tests:

r

```
test_that("functionName works correctly", {
    expect_equal(functionName(input1, input2),
expected_output)
    expect_error(functionName(bad_input1, bad_input2))
})
```

6. Build and Install the Package

- Check the package for errors and warnings:

r

```
devtools::check()
```

- Build the package:

r

```
devtools::build()
```

- Install the package locally:

```r
      devtools::install()
```

7. Version Control with Git

- Initialize a Git repository:

```r
      usethis::use_git()
```

- Add all files and commit:

```sh
      git add .
      git commit -m "Initial commit"
```

- Optionally, connect to a GitHub repository:

```r
      usethis::use_github()
```

8. Continuous Integration

- Set up GitHub Actions for automated testing:

```r
      usethis::use_github_action("check-standard")
```

- This ensures that your package is automatically tested on different R versions whenever you push changes.

9. Create a README and Vignettes

- Add a README file:

```r
      usethis::use_readme_rmd()
```

- Write vignettes to provide detailed examples:

```r
    usethis::use_vignette("introduction")
```

  - After editing the vignette, build it:

```r
    devtools::build_vignettes()
```

10. **Release Your Package**

  - Finalize documentation and ensure all checks pass:

```r
    devtools::document()
    devtools::check()
```

  - Submit to CRAN or share via GitHub:

```r
    devtools::release()
```

Advanced Data Manipulation Exercises

1. Implement Advanced Joins with Multiple Keys

Combine datasets using multiple keys to perform more precise joins. This exercise focuses on utilizing `dplyr`'s join functions (`inner_join`, `left_join`, `right_join`, `full_join`) with multiple columns as keys.

  Steps:

  - Load two related datasets that share more than one common column.

  - Use `inner_join()` to merge the datasets based on multiple keys.

  - Explore `left_join()`, `right_join()`, and `full_join()` to understand how they handle non-matching rows.

```r
```

```r
library(dplyr)
# Sample datasets
df1 <- data.frame(
  ID = c(1, 2, 3, 4),
  Year = c(2020, 2021, 2020, 2021),
  Value = c(100, 200, 150, 250)
)
df2 <- data.frame(
  ID = c(2, 3, 4, 5),
  Year = c(2021, 2020, 2021, 2020),
  Description = c("A", "B", "C", "D")
)
# Inner Join on ID and Year
inner_join(df1, df2, by = c("ID", "Year"))
```

2. Manage Nested Data Structures with `tidyr` and `purrr`

Learn to handle nested data frames using `tidyr`'s `nest()` and `unnest()` functions combined with `purrr`'s mapping functions for complex data transformations.

Steps:

- Create a nested data frame grouping by a specific column.

- Apply a function to each nested group using `purrr::map()`.

- Unnest the transformed data back into a flat structure.

r

```r
library(tidyr)
library(dplyr)
library(purrr)
# Sample dataset
df <- tibble(
  Group = rep(c("A", "B"), each = 3),
  Value = 1:6
```

```r
)
# Nesting the data
nested_df <- df %>%
  nest(data = -Group)
# Applying a transformation to each group
transformed_df <- nested_df %>%
  mutate(data = map(data, ~ mutate(.x, Value_Squared =
Value^2)))
# Unnesting the data
transformed_df %>%
  unnest(data)
```

3. **Optimize Data Processing with** `data.table`

Utilize the `data.table` package for efficient data manipulation, especially with large datasets. This exercise demonstrates key `data.table` operations that can significantly speed up data processing tasks.

Steps:

- Convert a `data.frame` to a `data.table`.

- Perform filtering, grouping, and aggregating operations.

- Compare performance with equivalent `dplyr` operations.

```r
library(data.table)
library(dplyr)
# Sample dataset
df <- data.frame(
  ID = 1:1e6,
  Group = sample(LETTERS, 1e6, replace = TRUE),
  Value = rnorm(1e6)
)
# Convert to data.table
dt <- as.data.table(df)
```

```
# Data.table operations
system.time({
  dt_summary <- dt[, .(Mean_Value = mean(Value)), by = Group]
})
# Equivalent dplyr operations
system.time({
  df_summary <- df %>%
    group_by(Group) %>%
    summarize(Mean_Value = mean(Value))
})
```

4. Perform Data Normalization and Standardization

Apply normalization and standardization techniques to prepare data for analysis and modeling. This exercise covers scaling numerical variables to a common range or distribution.

Steps:

- Understand the difference between normalization and standardization.

- Use dplyr to apply scaling functions across multiple columns.

r

```
library(dplyr)
# Sample dataset
df <- data.frame(
  A = rnorm(100, mean = 50, sd = 10),
  B = runif(100, min = 0, max = 100),
  C = rpois(100, lambda = 20)
)
# Standardization (z-score)
df_standardized <- df %>%
  mutate(across(everything(), ~ scale(.) %>% as.vector()))
# Min-Max Normalization
df_normalized <- df %>%
```

```
mutate(across(everything(), ~ (.-min(.)) / (max(.) - min(.))))
```

5. Implement Window Functions with `dplyr`

Utilize window functions to perform calculations across a set of table rows related to the current row. This exercise demonstrates functions like `lag()`, `lead()`, `cumsum()`, and `cummean()`.

Steps:

- Use `lag()` and `lead()` to access previous and next row values.

- Calculate cumulative sums and means within groups.

r
```r
library(dplyr)
# Sample dataset
df <- data.frame(
  Group = rep(c("A", "B"), each = 5),
  Value = c(10, 20, 30, 40, 50, 15, 25, 35, 45, 55)
)
# Applying window functions
df_window <- df %>%
  group_by(Group) %>%
  arrange(Value) %>%
  mutate(
    Previous_Value = lag(Value, 1),
    Next_Value = lead(Value, 1),
    Cumulative_Sum = cumsum(Value),
    Cumulative_Mean = cummean(Value)
  )
```

6. Handle Hierarchical Data with `hierarchical clustering`

Manipulate and analyze hierarchical data structures using clustering techniques. This exercise focuses on creating and visualizing hierarchical clusters.

Steps:

- Perform hierarchical clustering on a dataset.

- Use dendrograms to visualize the clustering process.

r

```r
library(dplyr)
# Sample dataset
df <- mtcars[, c("mpg", "disp", "hp", "wt")]
# Calculate distance matrix
dist_matrix <- dist(df)
# Hierarchical clustering
hc <- hclust(dist_matrix, method = "complete")
# Plot dendrogram
plot(hc, labels = rownames(df), main = "Hierarchical Clustering Dendrogram")
```

7. Advanced Filtering with Multiple Conditions

Apply complex filtering criteria to datasets using multiple logical conditions. This exercise emphasizes combining `filter()` with &, |, and %in% operators for refined data selection.

Steps:

- Filter rows based on multiple conditions using logical AND (&) and OR (|).

- Utilize %in% for matching multiple values.

r

```r
library(dplyr)
# Sample dataset
df <- data.frame(
  ID = 1:100,
  Category = sample(c("A", "B", "C"), 100, replace = TRUE),
  Score = rnorm(100, mean = 75, sd = 10),
  Passed = sample(c(TRUE, FALSE), 100, replace = TRUE)
)
```

```
# Advanced filtering
filtered_df <- df %>%
  filter(
    (Category == "A" & Score > 80) |
    (Category %in% c("B", "C") & Passed == TRUE)
  )
```

8. Perform Data Sampling and Stratification

Execute sampling techniques to create representative subsets of data. This exercise covers random sampling, stratified sampling, and handling imbalanced datasets.

Steps:

- Perform simple random sampling using `sample_n()` and `sample_frac()`.

- Implement stratified sampling with `group_by()` and `sample_n()`.

r

```
library(dplyr)
# Sample dataset
df <- data.frame(
  Group = rep(c("Control", "Treatment"), each = 500),
  Outcome = rbinom(1000, 1, 0.5)
)
# Simple random sampling
random_sample <- df %>%
  sample_n(100)
# Stratified sampling
stratified_sample <- df %>%
  group_by(Group) %>%
  sample_n(100)
```

9. Manage and Transform Hierarchical Data with `jsonlite`

Convert and manipulate hierarchical data structures such as JSON using the `jsonlite` package. This exercise demonstrates parsing, modifying, and flattening JSON data.

Steps:

- Read JSON data into R using `fromJSON()`.

- Navigate and modify nested lists or data frames.

- Flatten hierarchical data for easier analysis.

r

```
library(jsonlite)
# Sample JSON data
json_data <- '{
  "employees": [
    {"name": "John", "department": "Sales", "age": 30},
    {"name": "Jane", "department": "HR", "age": 25},
    {"name": "Doe", "department": "IT", "age": 35}
  ]
}'
# Parse JSON
data_parsed <- fromJSON(json_data)
# Access and modify data
employees <- data_parsed$employees
employees <- employees %>%
  mutate(age_group = case_when(
    age < 30 ~ "Young",
    age >= 30 & age < 35 ~ "Mid-age",
    TRUE ~ "Senior"
  ))
# Flatten JSON
flattened_data <- fromJSON(json_data, flatten = TRUE)
```

10. Implement Data Imputation Techniques for Missing Values

Address missing data by applying various imputation methods. This exercise explores simple and advanced techniques to handle NA values effectively.

Steps:

- Identify missing values using `is.na()`.

- Apply mean/median imputation for numerical data.

- Use mode imputation or predictive modeling for categorical data.

r

```r
library(dplyr)
# Sample dataset with missing values
set.seed(123)
df <- data.frame(
  ID = 1:50,
  Score = c(rnorm(45, mean = 75, sd = 10), rep(NA, 5)),
  Category = sample(c("A", "B", "C", NA), 50, replace = TRUE)
)
# Mean imputation for numerical data
df <- df %>%
  mutate(Score = ifelse(is.na(Score), mean(Score, na.rm = TRUE), Score))
# Mode imputation for categorical data
mode_category <- names(sort(table(df$Category), decreasing = TRUE))[1]
df <- df %>%
  mutate(Category = ifelse(is.na(Category), mode_category, Category))
```

11. Create Custom Data Manipulation Functions with purrr

Develop reusable functions to perform complex data manipulations using the purrr package. This exercise highlights the power of functional programming in R for efficient data processing.

Steps:

- Write a custom function to apply a series of transformations.

- Use `purrr::map()` to apply the function across a list or vector.

r

```
library(dplyr)
library(purrr)
# Custom function to scale and center data
scale_center <- function(df) {
  df %>%
    mutate(across(where(is.numeric), ~ scale(.) %>%
as.vector()))
}
# Sample list of data frames
list_of_dfs <- list(
  df1 = data.frame(A = rnorm(10), B = rnorm(10)),
  df2 = data.frame(A = rnorm(10), B = rnorm(10))
)
# Apply the custom function to each data frame in the list
scaled_list <- map(list_of_dfs, scale_center)
```

12. Handle Time-Lagged Data Operations

Perform operations that depend on previous or future data points, such as calculating growth rates or moving averages. This exercise emphasizes the use of lagged variables for time-series analysis.

Steps:

- Use `lag()` to create time-lagged variables.

- Calculate growth rates or moving averages based on lagged data.

r

```
library(dplyr)
# Sample time-series dataset
df <- data.frame(
  Quarter = 1:8,
  Revenue = c(100, 150, 130, 170, 160, 180, 200, 220)
)
```

```r
# Calculate quarter-over-quarter growth rate
df <- df %>%
  mutate(
    Revenue_Lag1 = lag(Revenue, 1),
    Growth_Rate = (Revenue - Revenue_Lag1) / Revenue_Lag1 * 100
  )
# Calculate 3-quarter moving average
df <- df %>%
  mutate(
    Moving_Avg_3Q = (Revenue + lag(Revenue, 1) + lag(Revenue,
2)) / 3
  )
```

13. **Perform Data Reshaping with** `melt` and `cast` from `reshape2`

Reshape data between wide and long formats using the `reshape2` package's `melt()` and `cast()` functions. This exercise is crucial for preparing data for various types of analyses and visualizations.

Steps:

- Convert a wide-format data frame to long format using `melt()`.

- Reshape the long-format data back to wide format using `dcast()`.

r
```r
library(reshape2)
# Sample wide-format dataset
wide_df <- data.frame(
  ID = 1:3,
  Jan_Sales = c(100, 150, 200),
  Feb_Sales = c(120, 160, 210),
  Mar_Sales = c(130, 170, 220)
)
# Melt to long format
long_df <- melt(wide_df, id.vars = "ID",
```

```r
                    variable.name = "Month", value.name = "Sales")
# Clean Month names
long_df$Month <- gsub("_Sales", "", long_df$Month)
# Cast back to wide format
reshaped_df <- dcast(long_df, ID ~ Month, value.var = "Sales")
```

14. Implement Data Validation and Cleaning Pipelines

Create robust data validation and cleaning workflows to ensure data integrity before analysis. This exercise covers identifying anomalies, enforcing data types, and applying custom validation rules.

Steps:

- Define validation rules for each column.

- Apply checks and handle violations using `dplyr` and conditional statements.

r
```r
library(dplyr)
# Sample dataset with potential issues
df <- data.frame(
  ID = 1:10,
  Age = c(25, 30, -5, 40, 50, 120, 35, 28, 60, NA),
  Email = c("user1@example.com", "user2@example",
"user3@example.com",
          "user4@.com", "user5@example.com", "user6@example.com",
          "user7example.com", "user8@example.com",
"user9@example.com", "user10@example.com")
)
# Validation pipeline
df_clean <- df %>%
  # Remove rows with invalid Age
  filter(Age > 0 & Age < 100) %>%
  # Ensure Email has a valid format
```

```r
    filter(grepl("^[A-Za-z0-9._%+-]+@[A-Za-z0-9.-]+\\.[A-Za-z]
{2,}$", Email))
```

15. Integrate External APIs for Data Retrieval and Manipulation

Fetch and manipulate data from external APIs using packages like `httr` and `jsonlite`. This exercise demonstrates how to interact with web services and incorporate external data into your workflows.

Steps:

- Make GET requests to an API endpoint.

- Parse and process the retrieved JSON data.

- Integrate the API data with existing datasets.

r

```r
    library(httr)
    library(jsonlite)
    library(dplyr)
    # Example API: OpenWeatherMap (Replace 'YOUR_API_KEY' with a
valid key)
    api_key <- "YOUR_API_KEY"
    city <- "New York"
    url <- paste0("http://api.openweathermap.org/data/2.5/weather?
q=",
                  city, "&appid=", api_key, "&units=imperial")
    # Make GET request
    response <- GET(url)
    # Check if the request was successful
    if (status_code(response) == 200) {
      # Parse JSON content
      weather_data <- content(response, "text") %>%
        fromJSON()
      # Extract relevant information
      weather_df <- tibble(
```

```r
      City = weather_data$name,
      Temperature = weather_data$main$temp,
      Humidity = weather_data$main$humidity,
      Weather = weather_data$weather[[1]]$description
    )
    print(weather_df)
  } else {
    print("Failed to retrieve data from API.")
  }
```

16. Develop Complex Data Transformation Pipelines with `magrittr`

Utilize the `%>%` pipe operator to create readable and maintainable data transformation pipelines. This exercise emphasizes chaining multiple operations seamlessly.

Steps:

- Combine multiple `dplyr` functions into a single pipeline.

- Incorporate conditional transformations and custom functions within the pipeline.

r
```r
    library(dplyr)
    library(magrittr)
    # Sample dataset
    df <- data.frame(
      ID = 1:100,
      Score = rnorm(100, mean = 70, sd = 15),
      Group = sample(c("Control", "Treatment"), 100, replace =
TRUE)
    )
    # Complex transformation pipeline
    transformed_df <- df %>%
      filter(Score > 50) %>%
      mutate(
        Grade = case_when(
```

```r
      Score >= 90 ~ "A",
      Score >= 80 ~ "B",
      Score >= 70 ~ "C",
      Score >= 60 ~ "D",
      TRUE ~ "F"
    )
  ) %>%
  group_by(Group, Grade) %>%
  summarize(Count = n(), Average_Score = mean(Score)) %>%
  arrange(Group, desc(Count))
```

17. Handle Missing Data in Time-Series with zoo

Address missing values in time-series data using the zoo package's interpolation and filling methods. This exercise focuses on preserving temporal integrity while imputing missing observations.

Steps:

- Identify missing timestamps in the time-series data.

- Apply linear interpolation or other methods to estimate missing values.

r

```r
  library(zoo)
  library(dplyr)
  # Sample time-series data with missing months
  dates <- as.Date(c("2021-01-01", "2021-02-01", "2021-04-01",
"2021-05-01"))
  values <- c(100, 150, 200, 250)
  ts_df <- data.frame(Date = dates, Value = values)
  # Create a complete date sequence
  complete_dates <- data.frame(Date = seq.Date(from =
as.Date("2021-01-01"),
                                               to =
as.Date("2021-05-01"), by = "month"))
```

```r
# Merge and identify missing values
ts_complete <- complete_dates %>%
  left_join(ts_df, by = "Date") %>%
  arrange(Date)
# Apply linear interpolation
ts_complete$Value_Imputed <- na.approx(ts_complete$Value, na.rm
= FALSE)
```

18. Implement Data Aggregation with Grouping and Nesting

Perform advanced data aggregation by grouping data into nested structures and applying customized summary functions. This exercise leverages `dplyr`'s `group_by()` and `nest()` functions for flexible aggregations.

Steps:

- Group data by one or more categorical variables.

- Nest the grouped data and apply summary statistics to each group.

r

```r
library(dplyr)
library(tidyr)
# Sample dataset
df <- mtcars %>%
  rownames_to_column(var = "Car") %>%
  select(Car, cyl, gear, mpg, hp)
# Grouping and nesting
grouped_df <- df %>%
  group_by(cyl, gear) %>%
  nest()
# Applying summary function to each group
summarized_df <- grouped_df %>%
  mutate(
    mpg_mean = map_dbl(data, ~ mean(.x$mpg)),
    hp_sum = map_dbl(data, ~ sum(.x$hp))
```

```
    ) %>%
    select(-data)
```

19. Create and Utilize Custom Pivot Functions

Develop custom functions to pivot data dynamically based on varying requirements. This exercise enhances the ability to reshape data efficiently using tidyr's pivot_longer() and pivot_wider() functions.

Steps:

- Write a function that takes parameters to determine pivoting behavior.

- Apply the function to different datasets with varying structures.

r

```r
library(tidyr)
library(dplyr)
# Custom pivot function
custom_pivot <- function(data, pivot_type = "long", ids,
names_from, values_from) {
    if (pivot_type == "long") {
        return(data %>% pivot_longer(cols = all_of(names_from),
                                     names_to = "Variable",
                                     values_to = "Value"))
    } else if (pivot_type == "wide") {
        return(data %>% pivot_wider(names_from =
all_of(names_from),
                                    values_from =
all_of(values_from)))
    } else {
        stop("Invalid pivot_type. Choose 'long' or 'wide'.")
    }
}
# Sample wide-format dataset
wide_df <- data.frame(
```

```
   ID = 1:3,
   Time1 = c(10, 20, 30),
   Time2 = c(15, 25, 35),
   Time3 = c(20, 30, 40)
)
# Pivot to long format
long_df <- custom_pivot(wide_df, pivot_type = "long",
                        names_from = c("Time1", "Time2", "Time3"),
                        values_from = "Value")
# Pivot back to wide format (assuming appropriate data structure)
# Note: This example assumes 'Variable' and 'Value' columns exist
# wide_df_reconstructed <- custom_pivot(long_df, pivot_type = "wide",
#                                       names_from = "Variable",
#                                       values_from = "Value")
```

20. Integrate and Manipulate Data from Multiple Sources

Combine data from various sources, such as databases, CSV files, and APIs, ensuring consistency and integrity across the merged dataset. This exercise emphasizes the challenges and techniques involved in consolidating heterogeneous data.

Steps:

- Import data from different formats and sources.

- Harmonize data types and structures.

- Merge the datasets using appropriate keys.

r

```
library(dplyr)
library(DBI)
library(readr)
```

```r
library(jsonlite)
# Importing CSV data
csv_data <- read_csv("data/sales_data.csv")
# Connecting to a database and retrieving data
con <- dbConnect(RSQLite::SQLite(), "data/database.sqlite")
db_data <- dbGetQuery(con, "SELECT * FROM customer_info")
dbDisconnect(con)
# Importing JSON data from an API
    api_response <- fromJSON("https://api.example.com/transactions")
api_data <- api_response$transactions
# Harmonizing column names and types
csv_data <- csv_data %>%
  rename(CustomerID = customer_id) %>%
  mutate(Date = as.Date(Date))
db_data <- db_data %>%
  rename(CustomerID = id) %>%
  mutate(JoinDate = as.Date(join_date))
api_data <- api_data %>%
  rename(CustomerID = cust_id, Amount = amount) %>%
  mutate(TransactionDate = as.Date(transaction_date))
# Merging datasets
merged_data <- csv_data %>%
  inner_join(db_data, by = "CustomerID") %>%
  left_join(api_data, by = "CustomerID")
```

CHAPTER 10

R Exercise for Data Mastery

1. Automate Data Import and Cleaning Pipeline

Streamline the process of importing and cleaning data by creating an automated pipeline. This exercise emphasizes the use of functions and scripting to handle repetitive tasks efficiently.

Steps:

- Define a function to read multiple CSV files from a directory.

- Apply cleaning operations within the function, such as handling missing values and renaming columns.

- Combine the cleaned data into a single data frame for analysis.

r

```r
library(dplyr)
# Function to read and clean individual CSV files
clean_csv <- function(file_path) {
  df <- read.csv(file_path)
  df <- df %>%
    rename(ID = id, Score = score) %>%
    mutate(Score = ifelse(is.na(Score), mean(Score, na.rm = TRUE), Score))
  return(df)
}
# Directory containing CSV files
```

```
file_dir <- "data/csv_files/"
# List all CSV files in the directory
file_list <- list.files(path = file_dir, pattern = "*.csv",
full.names = TRUE)
# Read and clean all CSV files, then combine them
combined_data <- lapply(file_list, clean_csv) %>%
  bind_rows()
head(combined_data)
```

2. Build a Custom Function for Summary Statistics

Create reusable functions to compute summary statistics, enhancing code modularity and efficiency. This exercise focuses on writing functions that can handle various data types and scenarios.

Steps:

- Define a function that calculates mean, median, and standard deviation for numeric columns.

- Incorporate error handling to manage non-numeric columns gracefully.

- Apply the function to different data frames to ensure versatility.

r

```
library(dplyr)
# Custom summary function
custom_summary <- function(df) {
  numeric_cols <- df %>% select(where(is.numeric))
  summary_df <- numeric_cols %>%
    summarize(across(everything(), list(
      Mean = ~ mean(.x, na.rm = TRUE),
      Median = ~ median(.x, na.rm = TRUE),
      SD = ~ sd(.x, na.rm = TRUE)
    ), .names = "{col}_{fn}"))
  return(summary_df)

}
```

```r
# Sample dataset
sample_df <- data.frame(
  Height = c(65, 70, 75, NA, 68),
  Weight = c(150, 160, 170, 180, NA),
  Age = c(25, 30, 35, 40, 45)
)
# Apply the custom summary function
summary_results <- custom_summary(sample_df)
print(summary_results)
```

3. Create an Interactive Dashboard with Shiny

Develop an interactive dashboard to visualize data dynamically. This exercise introduces the basics of the Shiny package, enabling the creation of user-friendly web applications for data exploration.

Steps:

- Set up the basic structure of a Shiny app with `ui` and `server` components.

- Incorporate input controls like sliders and dropdowns to filter data.

- Display reactive plots that update based on user input.

r

```r
library(shiny)
library(ggplot2)
# Sample dataset
data <- mtcars
# Define UI
ui <- fluidPage(
  titlePanel("MTCars Data Dashboard"),
  sidebarLayout(
    sidebarPanel(
      sliderInput("mpgRange", "Select MPG Range:",
                  min = min(data$mpg),
```

```r
                    max = max(data$mpg),
                    value = c(min(data$mpg), max(data$mpg))),
        selectInput("cylinders", "Select Cylinders:",
                    choices = unique(data$cyl),
                    selected = unique(data$cyl),
                    multiple = TRUE)
    ),
    mainPanel(
      plotOutput("mpgPlot")
    )
  )
)
# Define server logic
server <- function(input, output) {
  filtered_data <- reactive({
    data %>%
      filter(mpg >= input$mpgRange[1],
             mpg <= input$mpgRange[2],
             cyl %in% input$cylinders)
  })
  output$mpgPlot <- renderPlot({
    ggplot(filtered_data(), aes(x = wt, y = mpg)) +
      geom_point() +
      labs(title = "MPG vs Weight",
           x = "Weight (1000 lbs)",
           y = "Miles Per Gallon") +
      theme_minimal()
  })
}
# Run the application
shinyApp(ui = ui, server = server)
```

4. Develop a Data Transformation Pipeline Using dplyr

Construct a robust pipeline for transforming data using the `dplyr` package. This exercise highlights the sequential application of data manipulation functions to achieve complex transformations efficiently.

Steps:

- Utilize the pipe operator `%>%` to chain multiple `dplyr` functions.

- Perform operations such as filtering, mutating, grouping, and summarizing in a single pipeline.

- Ensure that each step logically builds upon the previous one to transform the data as required.

r

```r
library(dplyr)
# Sample dataset
sales_data <- data.frame(
    Region = rep(c("North", "South", "East", "West"), each = 5),
    Product = rep(c("A", "B"), times = 10),
    Revenue = c(200, 150, 300, 250, 400, 180, 220, 330, 270, 390,
210, 160, 310, 260, 420, 190, 230, 340, 280, 400)
)
# Data transformation pipeline
transformed_sales <- sales_data %>%
    filter(Revenue > 200) %>%
    mutate(Revenue_K = Revenue / 1000) %>%
    group_by(Region, Product) %>%
    summarize(Total_Revenue = sum(Revenue),
              Average_Revenue = mean(Revenue),
              .groups = 'drop') %>%
    arrange(desc(Total_Revenue))
print(transformed_sales)
```

5. Implement a Linear Regression Model

Build and evaluate a linear regression model to understand relationships between variables. This exercise covers model building, diagnostics, and interpretation of results using R's built-in functions.

Steps:

- Fit a linear model using the `lm()` function with appropriate predictors.

- Summarize the model to assess coefficients and significance levels.

- Visualize the model fit and residuals to evaluate assumptions.

r

```
library(ggplot2)
# Sample dataset
data(mtcars)
# Fit linear regression model
lm_model <- lm(mpg ~ wt + hp, data = mtcars)
# Summarize the model
summary(lm_model)
# Plot the residuals
ggplot(lm_model, aes(.fitted, .resid)) +
  geom_point() +
  geom_hline(yintercept = 0, linetype = "dashed", color = "red")
+
  labs(title = "Residuals vs Fitted",
      x = "Fitted Values",
      y = "Residuals") +
  theme_minimal()
```

6. Perform Text Analysis on a Dataset

Analyze textual data to extract meaningful insights using text mining techniques. This exercise introduces basic text processing, sentiment analysis, and visualization of word frequencies.

Steps:

- Load and preprocess text data using the `tm` package.

- Create a term-document matrix to quantify word occurrences.

- Generate a word cloud to visualize the most frequent terms.

r

```
library(tm)
library(wordcloud)
# Sample text data
text_data <- c(
  "R is a powerful tool for data analysis.",
  "Data visualization enhances data comprehension.",
  "Statistical modeling is essential for predictive analytics.",
  "Machine learning algorithms can uncover hidden patterns."
)
# Create a text corpus
corpus <- Corpus(VectorSource(text_data))
# Preprocess the text
corpus <- corpus %>%
  tm_map(content_transformer(tolower)) %>%
  tm_map(removePunctuation) %>%
  tm_map(removeNumbers) %>%
  tm_map(removeWords, stopwords("english")) %>%
  tm_map(stripWhitespace)
# Create Term-Document Matrix
tdm <- TermDocumentMatrix(corpus)
matrix <- as.matrix(tdm)
word_freq <- sort(rowSums(matrix), decreasing = TRUE)
df_word_freq <- data.frame(word = names(word_freq), freq =
word_freq)
# Generate word cloud
wordcloud(words = df_word_freq$word, freq = df_word_freq$freq,
```

```
                      min.freq = 1, max.words = 50, random.order = FALSE,
                  colors = brewer.pal(8, "Dark2"))
```

7. Optimize Code with Vectorization

Enhance the performance of your R scripts by leveraging vectorized operations. This exercise contrasts vectorized code with loop-based approaches, illustrating the efficiency gains achievable through vectorization.

Steps:

- Identify repetitive computations that can be vectorized.

- Rewrite loop-based code using vectorized functions like `apply()`, `sapply()`, or direct vector operations.

- Compare the execution time of both approaches to quantify performance improvements.

r
```
# Sample dataset
set.seed(123)
large_vector <- rnorm(1e6)
# Loop-based computation: calculating squared values
system.time({
  squared_values_loop <- numeric(length(large_vector))
  for (i in 1:length(large_vector)) {
    squared_values_loop[i] <- large_vector[i]^2
  }
})
# Vectorized computation
system.time({
  squared_values_vec <- large_vector^2
})
# Display a portion of the results
head(squared_values_vec)
```

8. Create a Function for Batch Plot Generation

Develop a custom function to generate multiple plots in a batch, facilitating repetitive visualization tasks. This exercise demonstrates how to encapsulate plotting logic within functions for reusability and scalability.

Steps:

- Define a function that accepts data and plotting parameters as arguments.

- Use the function to create and save multiple plots based on different subsets or variables.

- Automate the saving process by specifying file paths and names within the function.

r

```r
library(ggplot2)
# Custom plotting function
batch_plot <- function(data, x_var, y_var, plot_title,
file_name) {
    p <- ggplot(data, aes_string(x = x_var, y = y_var)) +
      geom_point() +
      labs(title = plot_title, x = x_var, y = y_var) +
      theme_minimal()
    ggsave(filename = file_name, plot = p, width = 6, height = 4)
}
# Sample dataset
data(mtcars)
# Generate and save multiple plots
variables <- c("mpg", "hp", "wt")
for (var in variables) {
    batch_plot(
      data = mtcars,
      x_var = var,
      y_var = "mpg",
      plot_title = paste("MPG vs", var),
      file_name = paste0("plots/MPG_vs_", var, ".png")
```

```
    )
  }
```

9. Build and Document an R Package

Create a custom R package to organize and share your functions and data. This exercise guides you through setting up the package structure, writing functions, documenting them, and preparing the package for distribution.

Steps:

- Initialize a new package using `devtools` and `usethis`.

- Develop functions and include them in the package.

- Add documentation using `roxygen2` comments.

- Set up testing infrastructure with `testthat`.

r

```r
library(devtools)
library(usethis)
# Create a new package
usethis::create_package("path/to/your/customPackage")
# Navigate to the package directory
setwd("path/to/your/customPackage")
# Create a new R script for a function
usethis::use_r("calculate_mean")
# Define the function in R/calculate_mean.R
#' Calculate Mean of a Numeric Vector
#'
#' This function calculates the mean of a numeric vector,
excluding NA values.
#'
#' @param x A numeric vector.
#' @return The mean of the vector.
#' @export
calculate_mean <- function(x) {
```

282

```
  if (!is.numeric(x)) {
    stop("Input must be a numeric vector.")
  }
  mean(x, na.rm = TRUE)
}
# Document the package
devtools::document()
# Add dependencies
usethis::use_package("dplyr")
# Set up testing
usethis::use_testthat()
# Create a test file for calculate_mean
usethis::use_test("calculate_mean")
# Write tests in tests/testthat/test-calculate_mean.R
library(testthat)
library(customPackage)
test_that("calculate_mean works correctly", {
  expect_equal(calculate_mean(c(1, 2, 3, 4, 5)), 3)
  expect_equal(calculate_mean(c(NA, 2, 4)), 3)
  expect_error(calculate_mean(c("a", "b", "c")))
})
```

10. Develop a Time Series Forecasting Script

Create a script to forecast future values in a time series dataset. This exercise introduces time series decomposition, model fitting, and forecasting using the `forecast` package.

Steps:

- Load and preprocess time series data.

- Decompose the time series to identify trend and seasonality.

- Fit an ARIMA model and generate forecasts.

- Visualize the forecasted values alongside historical data.

```r
library(forecast)
library(ggplot2)
# Sample time series data: Monthly airline passengers
data(AirPassengers)
ts_data <- AirPassengers
# Decompose the time series
decomposed_ts <- decompose(ts_data)
plot(decomposed_ts)
# Fit ARIMA model
arima_model <- auto.arima(ts_data)
summary(arima_model)
# Generate forecasts for the next 12 months
forecasted_values <- forecast(arima_model, h = 12)
plot(forecasted_values)
# Convert forecast to data frame for ggplot
forecast_df <- data.frame(
  Time = time(forecasted_values$mean),
  Forecast = as.numeric(forecasted_values$mean),
  Lower = as.numeric(forecasted_values$lower[,2]),
  Upper = as.numeric(forecasted_values$upper[,2])
)
# Plot using ggplot2
autoplot(ts_data) +
  autolayer(forecasted_values, series = "Forecast") +
  labs(title = "AirPassengers Forecast",
       x = "Year",
       y = "Number of Passengers") +
  theme_minimal()
```

11. Implement a Supervised Machine Learning Model

Develop a supervised machine learning model to predict outcomes based on labeled data. This exercise guides you through data preparation, model training, evaluation, and making predictions using the caret package.

Steps:

- Load and preprocess the dataset, ensuring all necessary features are included.

- Split the data into training and testing sets using stratified sampling.

- Train a supervised model (e.g., Random Forest) using the training set.

- Evaluate the model's performance on the testing set.

- Make predictions on new data and interpret the results.

r

```r
library(caret)
library(randomForest)
# Sample dataset
data(iris)
# Set seed for reproducibility
set.seed(123)
# Split data into training and testing sets
train_index <- createDataPartition(iris$Species, p = 0.7, list = FALSE)
train_data <- iris[train_index, ]
test_data <- iris[-train_index, ]
# Train a Random Forest model
rf_model <- train(Species ~ ., data = train_data, method = "rf")
# Summarize the model
print(rf_model)
# Make predictions on the test set
predictions <- predict(rf_model, newdata = test_data)
# Evaluate model performance
confusion <- confusionMatrix(predictions, test_data$Species)
```

```
print(confusion)
```

12. Create a Shiny Application for Interactive Data Exploration

Build a Shiny application that allows users to interactively explore and visualize data. This exercise covers setting up the UI and server components, integrating user inputs, and displaying dynamic outputs.

Steps:

- Define the user interface with input controls and output displays.

- Implement server logic to respond to user inputs and generate visualizations.

- Connect the UI and server to create a functional Shiny app.

- Test the application to ensure responsiveness and functionality.

r

```r
library(shiny)
library(ggplot2)
library(dplyr)
# Sample dataset
data(mtcars)
# Define UI
ui <- fluidPage(
  titlePanel("Interactive MTCars Explorer"),
  sidebarLayout(
    sidebarPanel(
      selectInput("xvar", "Select X-axis Variable:",
                  choices = names(mtcars)[sapply(mtcars,
is.numeric)],
                  selected = "wt"),
      selectInput("yvar", "Select Y-axis Variable:",
                  choices = names(mtcars)[sapply(mtcars,
is.numeric)],
                  selected = "mpg"),
```

```
        checkboxInput("show_fit", "Show Regression Line", value =
FALSE)
      ),
      mainPanel(
        plotOutput("scatterPlot")
      )
    )
  )
  # Define server logic
  server <- function(input, output) {
    output$scatterPlot <- renderPlot({
      p <- ggplot(mtcars, aes_string(x = input$xvar, y =
input$yvar)) +
        geom_point() +
        labs(title = paste(input$yvar, "vs", input$xvar),
           x = input$xvar,
           y = input$yvar) +
        theme_minimal()
      if (input$show_fit) {
        p <- p + geom_smooth(method = "lm", se = FALSE, color =
"blue")
      }
      print(p)
    })
  }
  # Run the application
  shinyApp(ui = ui, server = server)
```

13. Optimize Data Processing with Parallel Computing

Enhance the efficiency of data processing tasks by leveraging parallel computing techniques. This exercise demonstrates how to utilize multiple CPU cores to accelerate computations using the `parallel` package.

Steps:

- Set up a parallel backend using available cores.

- Export necessary data and functions to the worker nodes.

- Apply parallel processing to perform computationally intensive tasks.

- Collect and combine the results from all workers.

- Clean up the parallel environment after processing.

r

```r
library(parallel)
# Detect the number of available cores
num_cores <- detectCores() - 1
cl <- makeCluster(num_cores)
# Sample function to perform a time-consuming calculation
heavy_computation <- function(x) {
  Sys.sleep(1)   # Simulate a delay
  return(x^2)
}
# Export the function to the cluster
clusterExport(cl, varlist = "heavy_computation")
# Sample data
data_vector <- 1:10
# Perform parallel computation
system.time({
  results <- parLapply(cl, data_vector, heavy_computation)
})
# Stop the cluster
stopCluster(cl)
print(results)
```

14. Develop a Custom Data Validation Function

Create a function to validate data according to specific rules, ensuring data integrity before analysis. This exercise focuses on defining validation criteria and handling data that fails to meet these standards.

Steps:

- Define validation rules for each column in the dataset.

- Implement checks within a custom function to assess each rule.

- Flag or remove rows that do not comply with the validation criteria.

- Apply the validation function to clean and prepare the data for analysis.

r

```r
library(dplyr)
# Custom data validation function
validate_data <- function(df) {
  df_valid <- df %>%
    filter(
      Age > 0 & Age < 100,                          # Age must be
between 1 and 99
      !is.na(Email) & grepl("^[A-Za-z0-9._%+-]+@[A-Za-z0-9.-]+\
\.[A-Za-z]{2,}$", Email)  # Valid email format
    )
  return(df_valid)
}
# Sample dataset with potential issues
df <- data.frame(
  ID = 1:10,
  Age = c(25, 30, -5, 40, 50, 120, 35, 28, 60, NA),
  Email = c("user1@example.com", "user2@example",
"user3@example.com",
            "user4@.com", "user5@example.com",
"user6@example.com",
            "user7example.com", "user8@example.com",
"user9@example.com", "user10@example.com")
```

```
    )
    # Apply the validation function
    df_clean <- validate_data(df)
    print(df_clean)
```

15. Integrate External APIs for Data Retrieval

Fetch and incorporate data from external APIs into your R workflows. This exercise showcases how to make HTTP requests, parse JSON responses, and merge API data with existing datasets using the `httr` and `jsonlite` packages.

Steps:

- Choose an external API and obtain any necessary authentication keys.

- Use the `httr` package to make GET requests to the API endpoints.

- Parse the JSON responses into R data structures using `jsonlite`.

- Clean and transform the API data as needed.

- Merge the external data with your existing datasets for comprehensive analysis.

r

```r
    library(httr)
    library(jsonlite)
    library(dplyr)
    # Example API: OpenWeatherMap (Replace 'YOUR_API_KEY' with a
valid key)
    api_key <- "YOUR_API_KEY"
    city <- "New York"
    url <- paste0("http://api.openweathermap.org/data/2.5/weather?
q=",
                    city, "&appid=", api_key, "&units=imperial")
    # Make GET request
    response <- GET(url)
    # Check if the request was successful
    if (status_code(response) == 200) {
```

```
# Parse JSON content
weather_data <- content(response, "text") %>%
  fromJSON()
# Extract relevant information
weather_df <- tibble(
  City = weather_data$name,
  Temperature = weather_data$main$temp,
  Humidity = weather_data$main$humidity,
  Weather = weather_data$weather[[1]]$description
)
print(weather_df)
} else {
print("Failed to retrieve data from API.")
}
```

16. Implement a Cross-Validation Workflow for Model Selection

Utilize cross-validation techniques to assess and select the best-performing machine learning models. This exercise leverages the `caret` package to perform k-fold cross-validation and compare different algorithms.

Steps:

- Define cross-validation parameters, such as the number of folds.

- Train multiple models using different algorithms with cross-validation.

- Compare model performance metrics to identify the optimal model.

- Select and finalize the best model for further analysis or deployment.

r

```
library(caret)
library(randomForest)
library(e1071)
# Sample dataset
data(iris)
```

```
# Define cross-validation settings
train_control <- trainControl(method = "cv", number = 5)
# Train a Random Forest model with cross-validation
rf_model <- train(Species ~ ., data = iris, method = "rf",
                    trControl = train_control)
# Train a Support Vector Machine model with cross-validation
svm_model <- train(Species ~ ., data = iris, method =
"svmLinear",
                    trControl = train_control)
# Compare model performances
results <- resamples(list(RandomForest = rf_model, SVM =
svm_model))
summary(results)
# Visualize model comparison
dotplot(results)
```

17. Create a Script for Automated Reporting with R Markdown

Develop an R Markdown script to generate dynamic and reproducible reports. This exercise demonstrates how to integrate code, visualizations, and narrative text to produce comprehensive analyses automatically.

Steps:

- Set up an R Markdown document with YAML header specifying output format.

- Embed R code chunks to perform data analysis and generate plots.

- Use narrative text to explain findings and insights.

- Customize the appearance and layout of the report.

- Knit the R Markdown document to produce the final report in desired format (e.g., HTML, PDF).

```markdown
---
title: "Automated Data Analysis Report"
author: "Your Name"
```

```
date: "r Sys.Date()"
output: html_document
---
```

```
{r setup, include=FALSE}
knitr::opts_chunk$set(echo = TRUE)
library(dplyr)
library(ggplot2)
```

Introduction

This report provides an automated analysis of the mtcars dataset, including summary statistics and visualizations.

Summary Statistics

```
{r summary-stats}
summary_stats <- mtcars %>%
  summarize(
    Average_MPG = mean(mpg),
    Median_HP = median(hp),
    Total_Cylinders = sum(cyl)
  )
print(summary_stats)
```

MPG Distribution by Cylinder Count

```
{r mpg-plot}
ggplot(mtcars, aes(x = factor(cyl), y = mpg)) +
  geom_boxplot(fill = "lightblue") +
  labs(title = "MPG Distribution by Cylinder Count",
       x = "Number of Cylinders",
       y = "Miles Per Gallon") +
  theme_minimal()
```

Conclusion

The analysis highlights the relationship between cylinder count and MPG, demonstrating how higher cylinder engines tend to have lower fuel efficiency.

18. Build a Real-Time Data Monitoring Tool

Create a tool to monitor and visualize data in real-time, enabling continuous tracking of key metrics. This exercise utilizes the `shiny` and `plotly` packages to develop an interactive dashboard that updates as new data becomes available.

Steps:

- Set up the Shiny app structure with UI for displaying real-time plots.

- Implement server logic to retrieve and process incoming data streams.

- Use reactive expressions to update visualizations dynamically.

- Enhance interactivity with features like zooming and tooltips using `plotly`.

- Deploy the application for continuous monitoring.

r

```r
library(shiny)
library(plotly)
library(dplyr)
# Simulate real-time data generation
generate_data <- function() {
  data.frame(
    Time = Sys.time(),
    Value = rnorm(1, mean = 50, sd = 10)
  )
}
# Define UI
ui <- fluidPage(
  titlePanel("Real-Time Data Monitoring"),
  mainPanel(
    plotlyOutput("realtimePlot")
```

```r
      )
    )
    # Define server logic
    server <- function(input, output, session) {
      # Initialize an empty data frame
      data <- reactiveVal(data.frame(Time =
as.POSIXct(character()), Value = numeric()))
      # Update data every second
      observe({
        invalidateLater(1000, session)
        new_entry <- generate_data()
        updated_data <- bind_rows(data(), new_entry)
        data(updated_data)
      })
      # Render the real-time plot
      output$realtimePlot <- renderPlotly({
        plot_ly(data(), x = ~Time, y = ~Value, type = 'scatter',
mode = 'lines+markers') %>%
          layout(title = "Live Data Stream",
                 xaxis = list(title = "Time"),
                 yaxis = list(title = "Value"))
      })
    }
    # Run the application
    shinyApp(ui = ui, server = server)
```

19. Optimize Database Queries with DBI and dplyr

Enhance the performance of database operations by integrating the DBI and dplyr packages. This exercise illustrates how to connect to a database, perform efficient queries, and manipulate data directly within R.

Steps:

- Establish a connection to the database using DBI.

- Use `dplyr` verbs to construct and execute SQL queries efficiently.

- Retrieve and manipulate the queried data within R.

- Ensure proper closure of the database connection after operations.

r

```r
library(DBI)
library(RSQLite)
library(dplyr)
# Connect to a SQLite database (or any other DB supported by DBI)
con <- dbConnect(RSQLite::SQLite(), dbname = "data/database.sqlite")
# Assume there is a table named 'customer_info'
# Retrieve data using dplyr
customer_data <- tbl(con, "customer_info") %>%
   filter(JoinDate >= as.Date("2020-01-01")) %>%
   select(CustomerID, Name, JoinDate, Country) %>%
   arrange(desc(JoinDate)) %>%
   collect()
print(head(customer_data))
# Disconnect from the database
dbDisconnect(con)
```

20. Implement Regular Expressions for Advanced Text Processing

Utilize regular expressions (regex) to perform complex text manipulations and extract valuable information from textual data. This exercise demonstrates pattern matching, extraction, and substitution techniques using the `stringr` package.

Steps:

- Define regex patterns to identify specific text structures or elements.

- Use `stringr` functions like `str_extract()`, `str_detect()`, and `str_replace()` to manipulate text.

- Apply regex operations to clean, transform, or extract data as needed.

- Validate the results to ensure accuracy of text processing.

r

```r
library(stringr)
library(dplyr)
# Sample text data
text_data <- c(
  "Contact us at support@example.com for assistance.",
  "Send an email to info@domain.org or sales@domain.org.",
  "Visit our website at https://www.example.com for more
information.",
  "Invalid email: user@@example..com"
)
# Extract valid email addresses
valid_emails <- str_extract_all(text_data,
  "[A-Za-z0-9._%+-]+@[A-Za-z0-9.-]+\\.[A-Za-z]{2,}")
print(valid_emails)
# Detect presence of URLs
has_url <- str_detect(text_data, "http[s]?://")
print(has_url)
# Replace email addresses with a placeholder
anonymized_text <- str_replace_all(text_data,
  "[A-Za-z0-9._%+-]+@[A-Za-z0-9.-]+\\.[A-Za-z]{2,}", "[EMAIL]")
print(anonymized_text)
```